Jim's Dedication
To Michele, Kennan and Erin, you guys make it all worthwhile.

IRONMAN® Triathlon Edition

Functional Strength for Triathletes

Exercises for Top Performance

Ingrid Loos Miller & Jim Herkimer

© Bakke-Svensson/Ironman

Meyer & Meyer Sport

Ironman®, 70.3® and M-Dot® are registered trademarks of World Triathlon Corporation.
Used here by permission.

Official Product of the Ironman® Triathlon

British Library Cataloguing in Publication Data
A catalogue record for this book is available from the British Library

Functional Strength for Triathletes
Maidenhead: Meyer & Meyer Sport (UK) Ltd., 2012
ISBN 978-1-84126-344-1

© 2012 by Meyer & Meyer Sport (UK) Ltd.
Auckland, Beirut, Budapest, Cairo, Cape Town, Dubai, Indianapolis,
Kindberg, Maidenhead, Sydney, Olten, Singapore, Tehran, Toronto
Member of the World
Sport Publishers' Association (WSPA)
www.w-s-p-a.org
Printed and bound by: B.O.S.S Druck und Medien GmbH, Germany
ISBN 978-1-84126-344-1
E-Mail: info@m-m-sports.com
www.m-m-sports.com

© Bakke-Svensson/Ironman

Contents

Editor's Note 7

Introduction 8

Chapter 1: What is Functional Strength Training?..10
- Triplanar Movement.. 11
- Enhancing Stability... 23
- Neuromuscular Enrichment 26
- How to Recognize Functional Exercises 27

Chapter 2: Why Every Triathlete needs Functional Strength Training........... 28
- The Blueprint Human 29
- Improved Endurance 30
- Injury Prevention... 31
- Longevity in the Sport 32
- Better Performance 32
- Overcoming Adversity 33
- Preventing Muscle Cramps.. 35

Chapter 3: Functional Strength Training Phases.................................... 36
- Corrective Phase for Balanced Strength 37
- Endurance Phase for Lasting Strength.................................. 39
- Power Phase for Fast Strength 39
- Time Off.. 40

Chapter 4: Sample FST Exercise Program 41
- Strength Training Warm-up.. 42
- Corrective Exercises 43
- Strength Exercises.. 52
- Endurance Strength Exercises 63
- Power Exercises.. 77

Chapter 5: Customize your FST Plan 86
- Step 1: Schedule the Training Phases 87
- Step 2: Choose the Exercises and
  Adjust Difficulty as Needed.. 88
- Step 3: Work FST into Your Training Schedule 92

Chapter 6: Equipment 95

Chapter 7: Injuries & Reconditioning 100

Chapter 8: Advanced Exercises... 105
- Integrating Motion 106
- Integrating Exercises for Swimming 112
- Integrating Exercises for Cycling 116
- Integrating Exercises for Running 119

Chapter 9: Ask the Expert... 121

Appendix A: Functional Strength Assessment.................................. 129

Editor's Note

Triathletes tend to be data hounds when it comes to measures of performance. They like big numbers when they look at their training hours, and small ones in body fat percentage and race times. They purchase all manner of devices to track their progress, but I would venture to guess that when it comes to the intricacies of anatomy and physiology, their eyes go glassy. The staples of every triathlete's dictionary, hip flexors, rotator cuff, and quadriceps are enough to help them identify areas that are tight, sore, or unfortunately, injured and that is sufficient.

The purpose of this book is not to make you an expert on anatomy. It is to give you tools that will help you achieve the numbers you care about. To that end, the terminology in this book is accurate, but not necessarily as detailed as it could be. We use less formal but common shorthand terms, like "abs" and "glutes," rather than spelling out every muscle in longhand every time.

Readers with a strong interest in anatomy and kinesiology are encouraged to do more research on the structure and function of the musculoskeletal system. Everyday triathletes who want to perform better with less downtime due to injury should simply read this book and follow the recommendations.

Introduction

John was referred to my office with persistent pain and weakness in his legs. He had completed multiple ultra distance triathlons and had been a competitive intercollegiate cross country runner in his youth. Now in his 50s, he was a competitive age group cyclist. He had given up triathlons and running a few years earlier because it made his back pain worse. The back pain had been going on for so long that he accepted it as normal for his age and didn't even mention it until he explained why he had turned to cycling. He was fine on the bike as long as he took 8-12 ibuprofen tablets during his long rides. John's athletic options were shrinking.

Because of his concerns about leg power and strength (he seemed resigned to the pill-popping), John enlisted the help of an excellent cycling coach who told him to start a weight lifting program. He went to the local gym and hired a personal trainer who put him to work on basic exercises like bench press, crunches, leg press, pull down, curls, knee extensions and leg curls. All of the exercises were on fancy machines that required John to sit or lay on a bench or otherwise position himself in a machine that isolated one muscle group at a time.

John's muscles got stronger. He was able to lift heavier weights on the machines, but his cycling didn't improve. I explained to him that traditional weight training is like building a bike out of premium components, but forgetting to connect them with high quality cables and a sturdy chain. The bike, like the body, only works when there is an effective connection between the power source (John) and the wheels. John's weight training had addressed some of the cycling muscles but it did nothing to improve the way his body functioned as a power generating machine. The weight lifting John did at the gym didn't help him transfer more power to the pedals.

The first thing we did was to fire his personal trainer and throw his weight room program out the window. Then we conducted a movement screen to evaluate his ability to balance, move and stabilize his body. John failed miserably; giving me the same look of shock and humiliation I have seen hundreds of times when a high-level athlete can't perform a relatively "simple" physical task.

I designed a targeted home strength program and John went to work on it. The program included exercises to make him strong as he moved in various directions (or planes, more on this later) and taught him the meaning of "core strength." He was amazed at how difficult the exercises were when he didn't have a bench to lay on or a machine to strap into. Instead he had to use his arms, legs, hips and torso together to keep his balance as he moved.

Three weeks later, John came back, and he was giddy as a kid in a candy store. He loved his new strength program. He was amazed at how quickly his nervous system responded, how soon he became stronger and how all of it translated into improved performance on the bike.

John's lack of "functional strength" had been responsible for most of his back pain and the corresponding weakness in his legs. With the new functional strength program, he was able to significantly reduce his medication (down to 1-2 ibuprofen intermittently during his long rides) and he was climbing hills better than ever.

Functional Strength Training (FST) is the key to improving athletic performance for every athlete. By eliminating imbalances and improving neuromuscular strength and coordination, training becomes more effective and the injury risk goes down.

John's story is not unique. It illustrates how the concept of strength training is misunderstood and misapplied, and likewise, how the right kind of strength program can change an athlete's life. This book is your shortcut to the results John experienced. Take the Functional Strength Assessment, customize the Functional Strength Plan, and start performing better today.

**The goal of a good strength training program
should not be about developing great success in the weight room.
It should be about transferring the gains developed in the weight room to
improved athletic performance.**

Chapter 1
What is Functional Strength Training?

© Bakke-Svensson/Ironman

Function: *The action for which a person or thing is specially fitted.*

Years ago, the idea of an endurance athlete in the weight room was absurd. The prevailing wisdom was that strength training for endurance athletes would result in big muscles and slow times. Flash forward to today. Boy, did we have it wrong! We now know so much more about the effects of strength on performance and on the intricate relationship between the nervous and musculoskeletal system that nowadays, the joke is on the endurance athlete who does not include strength training in his or her program.

But strength training isn't enough. It has to be the *right kind*. The right kind of resistance training engages the muscles and the nervous system in ways that enhance athletic performance. A 2008 study comparing traditional strength training with a more "functional" strength program demonstrated the superiority of the functional approach. Subjects who had done the 12-week functional program (called "free-form" in the study) improved measured strength 58% more and balance 196% more than those using traditional weight training (Spennewyn 2008).

This chapter will explain the three defining characteristics of Functional Strength Training (FST):

- Uses triplanar movement

- Develops stability in key areas of the body

- Enhances sport-specific neuromuscular function

Triplanar Movement

The exercises in traditional weight lifting programs require individual muscle groups to move back and forth in one directional plane. You push against a bar to do a "bench press" and pull a bar back toward yourself to "row." These are called *uniplanar* movements; they make individual muscles "stronger," but they don't help you swim, bike or run better.

Your body can be divided into the three planes pictured in Figure 1. The *sagittal* plane divides the right and left, the *frontal* plane divides front and back, and the *transverse* plane divides the top and bottom halves.

When you move forward, the structures of your body actually move in several directions at once. Just look at what happens when you run:

- Legs and arms move along the sagittal plane (front to back)

- Pelvis moves along the frontal plane (side to side), and

- Shoulders rotate and move along the transverse plane (twisting).

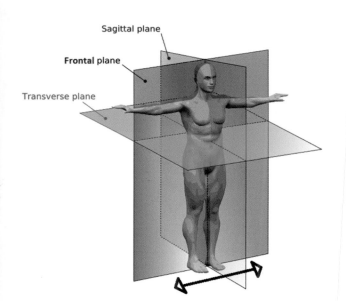

So we may think that we move in one direction when we run but actually we move in three directions (along 3 planes) simultaneously. The ability to execute and integrate these complex movements makes an athlete strong and fast.

Figure 1: The three planes of motion. The black arrow shows movement along the frontal plane.

Figure from "Sagittal plane" entry on Wikipedia.org.

The strength of any individual muscle is lost unless all of the needed muscles, structures and systems work effectively together to propel the body. Thus, the best way to improve strength is with exercises that challenge the body to work together in all three planes of motion. This triplanar movement is integral to FST.

Flexibility for Triplanar Motion

Motion, and therefore function, is impaired when muscles and other components of the musculoskeletal system are damaged, fatigued or respond poorly to nerve signals.

Limited flexibility means the muscles and connective tissues don't have full range of motion so extra force has to be applied to the muscle to get it moving. This extra force can damage the muscle fibers, pull joints out of alignment and cause a whole host of problems.

You probably know when your muscles are tight because you can feel it. But tightness can occur in other structures, too. For instance, tightness in the iliotibial (IT) band is common but you may not even realize you have it. The iliotibial band, a band of thick tissue that runs from the hip to just below the knee, can cause pain nearby in the hip or knee or farther away, in the low back.

To find out if you have flexibility problems that may affect performance, take the Functional Strength Test in Appendix A or have an evaluation conducted by a physical therapist familiar with the concepts of functional strength training. Problem areas can be addressed through the dynamic warm-up, active isolated stretching during cool down, or with self-myofascial release.

Dynamic Warm-up

Dynamic stretches are sport-specific movements, such as going forward or backward, side to side, rotating, or any combination of the three. Think of them as a series of funny walking maneuvers that ignite the neuromuscular system, increase the body's core temperature and get blood flowing to the muscles and connective tissues to prepare the body for action. Take about 10 "steps" of each one before you swim, bike and run.

Photo 1: Knee Hugs

Knee Hugs
While standing upright and balancing on the opposite ball of foot (calf raise), lift your knee up tight to the chest. Keep chest high, hold for one second, then step forward and switch legs.

The World's Greatest Stretch (WGS)

Step into a long lunge position with the right foot. Lean forward, bringing the right elbow to the inside of right ankle. Make sure to keep the back leg straight and hips pressed down to the ground to increase hip flexor stretch. Hold one second, then place your hands on the ground outside of the front leg and lift hips up, straightening the front leg while pulling the toes up toward the body. Make sure your hands are on the ground throughout the stretch. Hold one second, then step forward while switching the lead leg.

Photo 7: Back Lunge & Reach

Back Lunge and Reach

Step backwards into a long lunge position with the left foot and then rotate your body over the right leg. Keep your arms bent at 90°. Draw in your stomach while pushing your hips forward and hold for one second. Step back, switching legs and direction of rotation.

Photo 8: Inch Worm

Inch Worms

Keep your legs completely straight and reach down to the ground. Without moving your feet, walk your hands out as far as possible keeping your body tight and legs straight. Once fully stretched out, hold one second. Then slowly walk your feet in toward your hands, keeping your legs straight and raising your hips toward the sky, creating an upside down V (hold one second). Without getting up, walk your hands out again and repeat the exercise.

Active Isolated Stretching

Active isolated stretching (AIS) incorporates a stretching rope to gently assist pulling your muscle a little farther than normal for only 2 seconds at a time. The process is repeated up to 12 times. When used after exercise to cool down, this series of contract-relax stretches helps to reprogram the joint and muscle receptors to "remember" the new range of motion.

Photos 9,10 and 11 below show three AIS stretches that address range of motion problems in the hip and leg.

Photo 9: AIS Adductor

Photo 10: AIS Hamstring

Photo 11: AIS Quadriceps

Self-myofascial Release

Dysfunctional movement and feelings of tightness can originate from structures known as *fascia*. Found throughout the body, fascia are bands of dense connective tissue that help bind together muscle groups, blood vessels and nerves. The IT band is one example of a very thick band of fascia, but fascia of varying thickness but is found throughout the body. A white-colored sheath, fascia acts the "Saran wrap" of the body that helps to keep important structures intact and also helps to transmit movement from one segment to the next. Much like the roads we drive on, muscles covered with fascia form the pathways in which our muscles move.

If we overuse these pathways, the tissue can be traumatized and develop rough areas called *adhesions*, which are like speed bumps on a road. Adhesions can reduce the blood flow to muscles, cause dysfunction and contribute to poor performance. Some adhesions are very sensitive to irritation. These are known as *trigger points*.

Self-myofascial release is a form of massage that reduces the number and severity of these trigger points by applying varying levels pressure to them. Tools like foam rollers, massage sticks and balls of various size and firmness can be rolled over trigger points to literally smooth out the bumps. This stimulates blood flow, allows healing and improves function. When tightness eases and range of motion improves, pain will subside. The process of reducing trigger points can take days or weeks and once the area loosens up, you should continue to use rollers on it twice a week to keep the area supple.

Depending on the location and tenderness of the trigger point, pressure can be applied with body weight or by hand. To apply body weight, place a soft ball or roller under the affected limb. Roll your body back and forth over the ball from a point above the trigger point to slightly below it (see Photo 12). You can often feel the knot of tightness when you roll over it, and you can also feel it lessen or release. Using body weight is effective for the thighs, buttocks, hips, calves, and the back.

Photo 12: Using bodyweight to apply pressure to a trigger point

Foam rollers come in various sizes and levels of firmness. Start with a softer roller/lighter pressure and work your way up to a more rigid or textured roller like the one in Photo 13.

Photo 13: The texturing on The Grid roller from Triggerpoint will allow you to apply aggressive pressure. Photo provided by the manufacturer and used with permission.

When small, thinner muscles in the lower legs, forearms or shoulders need attention, pressure can be applied by hand rather than body weight. There are hand-held rollers and "sticks" on the market for this purpose (Photo 14).

Photo 14: "The Stick" massager is used to apply pressure to calf. Photo provided by manufacturer and used with permission.

A word of caution: Self-myofascial release is simple to do, but it can be quite painful, especially the first few times you do it. Apply enough pressure to make it "comfortably uncomfortable." However, the more often that you "roll out," the less discomfort you will feel. This is truly a "no pain, no gain" situation.

Enhancing Stability

Triplanar movement is an important concept, but motion is a little more complicated than that because when some parts of the body move in one direction, other parts need to hold fast and resist that motion. That resistance is known as *stability*, and it is a vital component of movement.

Once again we will use running to illustrate: The quicker your legs move and the more force you apply the ground, the faster you will run. You need to have *mobility* to move your legs forward and back. At the same time, your shoulders and pelvis need to have *stability* to resist the force that the legs direct to the ground. If your shoulders rotate too far or your pelvis moves too much, that energy will dissipate rather than being directed to the ground and you will not go as fast. Physical therapist Gray Cook calls these "energy leaks."

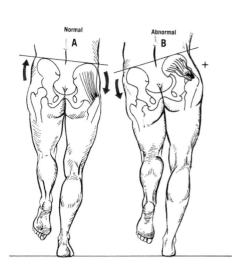

The runner (B) in Figure 2 has an energy leak because he has poor pelvic stability. In this case, the instability is caused by a weak gluteus medius muscle on the right side, which causes the left hip to drop. A program to strengthen that muscle and improve the stability of that kinetic chain will improve this runner's form, reduce the chance of injury, and allow him to run faster.

Figure 2: Runner B has poor pelvic stability

Image from online version of Basic Human Anatomy by O'Rahilly, Muller, Carpenter & Swensen at http://www.dartmouth.edu/~humananatomy/figures/chapter_18/18-3.HTMat.

Used with permission.

Triathletes need stability in the areas of the body that are transfer stations for power. For a swimmer, that means the core muscles and shoulders. The same areas must be stable for running and cycling to transfer power to the ground or to the pedals. This leads us to the concept of core stability.

What is core stability?

Developing "core stability" is becoming the mantra in fitness centers around the country. I often ask people what they mean by that term and they typically say "strong abdominals." While this answer is partially correct, it leaves out a number of other important muscles. Training your rectus abdominis (6-pack) muscle in isolation is ineffective in generating and channeling forces for athletic movement. An integrated, multi-dimensional program is necessary to fully activate all the components that make up the core.

Your "core" is your middle, foundation, or central part. Probably the best way to think of it is your center of gravity. It is located a couple of inches in front of your lower lumbar or upper sacral vertebra (low back). *Stability* means strength, solidity or firmness. So core stability is simply *strength around your center.*

The muscles that surround your core can be seen as a bowl. The core muscles are the bowl, and your vital organs are contained inside. The muscles in your pelvic floor form the bottom of the bowl and the sides of the bowl travel upward and include the gluteals, spine extensors, deep spine rotators, and

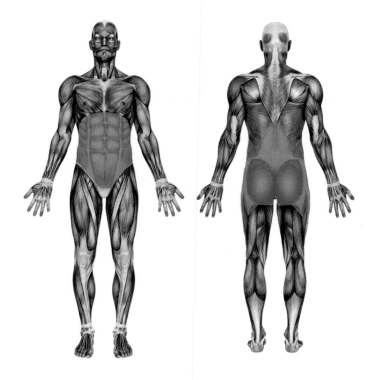

Figure 3:
Core Stability
Musculature

abdominals (see Figure 3). The diaphragm acts as the lid to the bowl and is one of the reasons that proper breathing plays a role in core stability. Keep in mind, there are four layers of abdominal muscles and for optimal core stability the deepest two layers, the ones that no one see (transverse abdominis and internal oblique,) are the are most important.

When the core muscles contract, they don't move limbs but rather tighten around you. This is known as the "serape" effect (1970 Logan & McKinney). A serape is a Mexican garment that is draped loosely about the shoulders and crosses in front of the body, much like a blanket. When the core muscles contract, they create rotational stability in the torso and generate force from the hip to the opposite shoulder. When you run, this action provides stability when your right arm swings forward as your left leg swings back. When you ride your bike, you have to hold the handlebars firmly with the right hand when the left leg pushes.

Maintaining a strong and functional core will limit the amount of stress on the ligaments and discs in your spine, reducing the risk of developing a chronic or overuse injury. Many overuse injuries that appear in the back, legs, and feet are due in large part to core instability.

Optimal Posture

The optimal position for the spine is mid-way between flexed (slouching) and extended (arched back). Maintaining this "neutral spine" position during athletic activities will maximize load transfer and minimize stress on the ligaments and discs.

Find your neutral spine position by standing up with your hands on your hips. Now push your belly forward (rotate pelvis) as far as it will go, arching your lower back. This will create an excessive lumbar extension curve that is too far. Now, pull your belly in as far as you can as you curl your pelvis (flex your spine). Lightly squeezing your glutes will help. This should create a flat lumbar spine, which is the other extreme position. Practice moving forward and back as far as possible until you can easily move through the full range of motion. Now stop halfway between the fully flexed and fully extended position. This should put the spine in a neutral position.

Neuromuscular Enrichment

Your brain constantly receives information from the body and the environment. This information is gathered in specialized nervous system receptors in the skin, muscle, joints and tendons, known as proprioceptors. If you put your arm behind your back, you can't see it, but you know it's there because of the information these little marvels send to your brain. But the communication operates unconsciously too, telling your brain whether and how fast your joints are moving, and how far and how forcefully muscles are being stretched and contracted. All of this occurs automatically. Indeed, proprioceptive memory is likely part of the "phantom limb" syndrome often experienced by amputees.

Your brain responds to input by sending signals down the spinal cord to nerves in muscles and the muscle responds. This information exchange between nerves and muscles is the neuromuscular system. This is an oversimplification because information is passed between other structures too, but we will just focus on brain to muscle communication here.

The more information that passes through this system, the finer tuned, less wasteful, and more efficient an athlete's movements will be, both on a conscious and unconscious level. In this way, we could say that a "smart" neuromuscular system transmits oodles of complex information in both directions and a "stupid" one handles only a limited amount. Couched in these terms, traditional strength training, which isolates muscles into a single plane of motion, does nothing to make your neuromuscular system "smarter" because it only stimulates communication in *one direction*, from brain to muscle.

Functional strength training, however, makes your neuromuscular system smarter because heaps of information are passed from muscle to brain and back again *(both directions)*. This two-way exchange provides many important benefits, but one of the most important for endurance athletes is improved work economy. An economical triathlete can swim, bike, and run faster for the amount of oxygen used than a less economical one. Work economy requires a "smart" neuromuscular system that works together with the cardiovascular system to maximize oxygen efficiency.

Your neuromuscular system also helps you maintain balance. Balance can be impaired with disuse, poor posture, muscle weakness, joint dysfunction, or following injury. It is not surprising that poor balance increases the risk of lower extremity injury in athletes (McGuine 2000).

Triathletes are constantly dealing with balance issues. Running and cycling are both highly complex processes of rapidly losing, regaining, and maintaining balance on alternating legs, yet we do it without even thinking about it.

Adding instability to the right kind of exercise makes it more effective because in addition to doing the movement against resistance, the body must also maintain balance. Indeed the first FST session can be both mentally and physically exhausting because keeping your balance requires intense focus and control. The challenge of doing so amplifies neuromuscular activity and necessitates active and ongoing engagement of the core muscles as you struggle to quit wobbling. With practice, your neuromuscular system adapts and the exercises get easier.

How to Recognize Functional Exercises

Now that you know a bit more about what FST is, you should learn to tell the difference between an exercise that is functional and one that isn't. This will prevent you from wasting your time on useless exercises. An exercise must satisfy these three requirements to be functional:

1. The exercise must allow movement in multiple planes; it must be triplanar.
2. The exercise must require stability through one or more transfer stations including the ankle, hip, core, or shoulder.
3. The exercise must engage kinetic chains that are used to swim, bike or run. For triathletes, this means single-leg propulsion and shoulder-to-hip rotation.

Below are examples of traditional weight training exercises that meet these criteria.

Some traditional non-functional exercises	Functional versions of the same exercise
Leg press machine	Single leg squat
Military or shoulder press machine	Single leg shoulder press with dumbbells
Push-ups and pull-ups are functional exercises	Push-ups with feet on Swiss ball or in suspension trainer are more functional
Hamstring curls on Machine	Hamstring curls using Swiss ball
Seated row on machine	Single leg standing row using cable
Calf raises on Machine	Single leg calf raises with hip rotation, holding a dumbbell
Sit-ups	Pikes with feet in a TRX suspension trainer

Chapter 2
Why Every Triathlete Needs Functional Strength Training

"Strength in sports should be viewed as the mechanism required to perform skills and athletic actions."

Tudor Bompa

The Blueprint Human

It is important to point out that you may have neuromuscular deficits that you are not even aware of. The perfect "Blueprint Human" has a perfectly balanced body structure and an intact neuromuscular system that executes normal movement patterns. Unfortunately, none of us is perfect but the super athletes are probably closest to this ideal.

Even without a history of injury or sloth, your genetics may be working against you becoming a standout swimmer, cyclist or runner. Add to this some life experience, lots of screen time, poor posture, wearing 4-inch high heels during your career phase, and maybe an injury that you had years ago. These events and many more can disrupt normal movement patterns, and our bodies have adjusted to them in subtle ways.

Over time, these compensations become ingrained neuromuscular patterns. These patterns affect muscle strength and function in ways that are not problematic until you challenge the system by taking up triathlon and even then, you can probably do all right for a while. When someone suggests you add strength training to your plan, you understandably, bristle.

Triathletes are aerobic animals that thrive on long, hypnotic bouts of motion. Pushing weight around takes you out of your comfort zone. It is intense, sweaty work, and it is understandable that you don't want to compromise the quality of the swim, bike and run sessions you hold dear.

But those little movement issues are still there, waiting.

Endurance training doesn't correct faulty movement patterns, and stressing imbalanced muscles doesn't even them out it. It does just the opposite, making the dysfunctions more pronounced and problematic.

The solution is specific strengthening and neuromuscular reeducation to make your body function more like the Blueprint Human. In fact, the right kind of program could make you even better than that. FST training will hone triathlon-specific strength and neuromuscular control that will propel you to the finish line better and faster than ever before.

Improved Endurance

It was once believed that strength and endurance training would interfere with each other, but this notion has been well studied and it turns out that it is false (Dudley and Fleck, 1987, Hickson, et. al., 1988; Sale, et. al., 1999, Tanaka 1998, Paavolanen 1999, Millet 2002, Hoff 2002)

If you are like most triathletes, you focus mostly on endurance training. You might even do some high-intensity intervals. This is all good, but this kind of training doesn't stimulate the kind of adpatations that a functional strength program will address.

Triathlon requires a combination of strength, speed, and endurance. The Performance Triangle (Figure 4) shows the biomotor abilities that are common to all sport. Soccer requires the same basic abilities as triathlon but the emphasis is different. Since endurance is the dominant ability for triathletes, that is where you should spend *most* of your training time. But most is not *all*. As the triangle shows, endurance does not stand alone; it coexists, and it is actually ehnanced by the other abilities. That is where functional strength training comes in.

Adding resistance training to your endurance program improves *endurance capacity* (Tanaka 1998). If you want to be a better endurance athlete, you must also develop muscle strength and anaerobic power. Likewise, if you neglect these two components, your endurance performance will never be developed to its full potential. This is important not only for elite athletes, but for newbies and age-groupers, too.

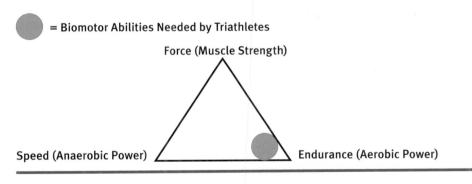

Figure 4: Performance Triangle showing abilities needed by triathletes. Adapted from Tudor Bompa's triangle of biomotor abilities.

Injury Prevention

Athletes who have been injured and rehabilitated with physical therapy understand something about the importance of functional strength. Physical therapy uses FST (and other things) to help patients return to normal movement patterns. FST for athletes takes this approach a step further. Like John, the cyclist described in the introduction, strength gaps occur even in athletes, and it is sad when choices are narrowed year after year because of injuries that could have been prevented or corrected with the right approach. I often tell people, "You should race for as long as you want to. Stop because you want to not because you are injured and your body makes you." Getting strong (and staying that way) will keep your options open.

It is well agreed that strength training protects you from injury by fortifying the entire musculoskeletal system, including the bones, muscles, and connective tissues. Reinforcing these structures is fundamental to your success because, as a triathlete, you do the same motions again and again for hours on end. Overuse injuries account for 80-85% of injuries to triathletes according to Sergio Migliorni, International Triathlon Union Medical Committee Chair. In one study, 155 British triathletes of various skill levels kept training diaries. Over the period of eight weeks, 37% of them reported sustaining an injury that they defined as a problem causing missed training, reduced mileage, or taking medication (Korkia 1994).

A 2010 analysis of triathlon injuries (Figure 5) shows various sites that are commonly injured in triathletes (Vleck 2010). It is unknown whether the triathletes in any of the various studies participated in a strength training program of any kind. Certainly, this is an area ripe for study.

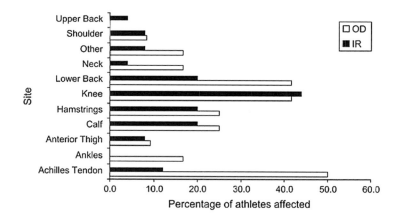

Figure 5: Triathlete Injuries (Vleck 2010).

The certainty of impending injury is something triathletes must come to terms with. Incorporating FST into your program will become important to every triathlete sooner or later. Get started now so you won't miss valuable training time later.

Longevity in the Sport

Men and women reach peak strength in their early to mid 20s, which then decreases at a rate of about 1% per year. We also lose about 10% of our aerobic capacity per decade. The age-related decline in performance is most pronounced in running and ultra triathlon distance races (Lepers 2010).

Aerobic capacity is not the only thing that suffers with age; movement speed, rate of force development, and power diminishes in time too. Fast-twitch muscle fibers decrease in size and number (faster than the decrease in slow-twitch fibers) and are replaced by fatty/fibrous tissue. Inactivity hastens the general deterioration of the nervous system.

The good news is that individuals who maintain a lifestyle of vigorous activity hold onto their athletic capacities far longer and deteriorate more slowly than this. It is truly a matter of "use it or lose it."

Functional strength training can slow the loss of aerobic capacity by optimizing muscularity and minimizing fat storage. Moreover, by reducing the rate of injury, training volume and intensity can be maintained longer.

Who says you can't get to Kona by outlasting everyone in your age group?

Better Performance

Developing all of the abilities in the Performance Triangle will help you achieve your performance potential. Even though your races are long endurance events, if you are strong enough to cover a short distance fast (have a speed reserve), you will be able to travel longer distances at lower speed more easily. Athletes who do nothing but endurance work ignore this concept and, in time, they actually lose muscle strength. This is often the case with athletes addicted to the ultra triathlon distance who race the distance repeatedly. Eventually, they experience diminishing returns on their training. Instead of improving, they get slower and slower. FST helps these athletes regain muscle power and get back on the road to getting faster.

When combined with endurance training, the right kind of strength training improves strength, power, running economy, and speed in every discipline (Girold 2006, Saunders 2006, Girold 2007, Aspenes 2009, Yamamoto 2008, Yamamoto 2010). The neuromuscular adaptations that come from strength training are keys to improving running economy, which, in trained athletes, is more predictive of performance than a high VO2 max. The lower leg muscles of economical runners seem better able to anticipate the foot strike and stiffen just enough to give the runner optimal spring. Just as a golf ball (which is firm) travels farther than a tennis ball (which is softer), functional strength training teaches the muscles, among other things, to be at optimal tension at the foot strike.

Overcoming Adversity

If you raced without adversity, you wouldn't need much power in order to get to the finish line. But races aren't like that and "just finishing" isn't good enough for most triathletes. Think of power as the ability to "step on the gas" and even if you aren't a podium chaser, there are times you need to be able to push harder.

During the swim start, getting quickly through the surf line (if there is one) is crucial if you want to avoid a thrashing. You need power for that. Wind and current will require higher energy output than your leisurely laps in the pool. You need to be able to accelerate around slower swimmers and to escape aggressive drafters who nip at your heels. You want to move swiftly around buoys and, at the end, you have to stand up and run as soon as you get to shore unless you want to be mowed over by those behind you.

You need power on the bike to zoom up the hills without losing too much speed. Hill climbing ability on the bike is determined mostly by the power-to-weight ratio of the cyclist. The best climbers carry 2 pounds of body weight per inch of height, so a 5'10" (178cm) cyclist will weigh a mere 140 pounds (64 kg). Functional strength training will improve power more than it will increase an athlete's weight.

Off-road triathletes need to generate much more power than road cyclists to ride over logs and boulders and handle to steep elevation changes. And don't forget the wind; you need power to sustain speed on a blustery day. Figure 6 shows just how much power is required to hold your speed on a bike in the wind.

There are also times when you need to pass other riders, because they are going too slow, you need to get out of the draft zone, or you want to avoid a mishap. USAT rules require athletes to pass within 20 seconds. You need power to pass other riders convincingly and also for "cat and mouse" games.

Studies on the effectiveness of strength training for cyclists are notably inconsistent in their methodology as it is unclear who is tested, what kind of "strength" training is used, and how results are measured. A systematic review and analysis of five of the best studies (Yamamoto 2010) showed that, indeed, the right kind of strength training improves maximal power and time trial performance.

Triathletes who routinely put in longer than four-hour training sessions hunched over a set of aero bars know that being strong on the bike means more than pedaling; it means being able to efficiently hold the aero position for hours, then stand up and run. You need strength for that.

Speaking of running, courses are never perfectly flat. There are curbs, hills, turns, obstacles, sand, wind, stairs (ouch), and other athletes to negotiate around. There is also ALWAYS a finish line. No matter what your race day brings, you want to be able to sprint across the finish line — or at least to cross it standing upright.

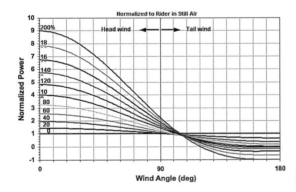

Figure 6: Power required for travel at constant speed on a bike, regardless of wind speed or direction. Retrieved from www.sheldonbrown.com/brandt/wind.html

Every triathlete has something to gain from functional strength: Improved endurance so you can go harder, longer. Injury prevention is important so you can keep training and continue to enjoy the health benefits of the sport. Everyone from beginners to elites can perform better. And finally, functional strength will help triathletes overcome the adversity we call "racing."

Preventing Muscle Cramps

Muscle cramps can be caused my many things, but a growing body of research suggests that exercise-induced muscle cramps (EAMC) are caused by impaired neuromuscular control in response to fatiguing exercise. A 2010 study reported on a triathlete and Ironman® triathlon competitor who suffered hamstring cramping during the run portion of the Ironman event. Testing showed dysfunctional movement patterns and muscle imbalances that were corrected over an 8-month period with a "functional" strength training program as we have defined it. Indeed, electromyogram (EMG) testing done before and after the exercise program confirmed that normal muscle activity was restored after the exercise program. After treatment, the athlete was able to race without hamstring cramping and reported personal best times (Wagner 2010).

The success of this intervention is consistent with epidemiological studies, experimental data and EMGs recorded during acute cramping following exercise (Sulzer 2005, Schweillinus 2007).

If you suffer from EAMC, you have everything to gain and nothing to lose by adding functional strength training to your program.

Chapter 3
Functional Strength Training Phases

A strong athlete has responsive muscles. Periodization is the progression of training phases originally developed for strength training and widely adopted for all athletic conditioning. Each phase is designed to enhance a particular element of athletic performance and prepare the athlete for the phase that follows. You have to be able to move through the entire range of motion without pain before you work on getting stronger, then you need to build strength so you can work on endurance, etc. The ultimate goal of this progression is to achieve a peak competitive performance.

Your periodized FST plan will improve performance by stimulating the body to adapt to sport-enhancing physical challenges. The intensity of these challenges is varied by changing the amount of resistance /weight, doing them on more or less stable surfaces, adding complexity to the movements, and, at some point, doing them faster.

Corrective Phase for Balanced Strength

The first phase of FST is designed to correct muscle imbalances, joint dysfunction, neuromuscular deficits, and distortions in postural patterns that an athlete may have developed over time. Some of these issues can also be genetic.

Simply by looking in the mirror you can see that as beautiful as you are, you are not completely symmetrical. This asymmetry applies to movement as much as it does to the placement of your facial features. Chances are that one side of your body is stronger, more coordinated and "athletic" than the other. These asymmetries are often subtle and go unnoticed, but large volumes of repetitive motion (swimming, cycling and running) bring imbalances and minor dysfunctions to the forefront.

Muscle strength and/or length imbalances set you up for overuse injuries. Consider your athletic history. Do you have persistent injuries? For example, does your right knee usually flare up at a certain point in training? Rest may temporarily reduce the pain, but it does not correct the underlying problem. Scar tissue forms on muscles and fascia, and posture and movement patterns may be altered. Failure to correct the underlying problem typically results in re-injury, sooner or later. Take the Functional Strength Assessment in Appendix A to find areas of weakness or get an evaluation from a physical therapist familiar with functional strength principles. Don't be surprised if you have issues that you weren't even aware of.

The amount of time you devote to the corrective phase depends upon where you are in your race season, the nature and extent of your areas of weakness, and how much time you have available. You may need up to six weeks in this phase to prepare you for what comes next. Ideally, this corrective work will be done in the off-season. Corrective exercises, however, can be incorporated into any phase of training as needed to keep problem areas at bay. Relatively low weights and a high number of repetitions are used so you can focus on keeping your balance and moving smoothly.

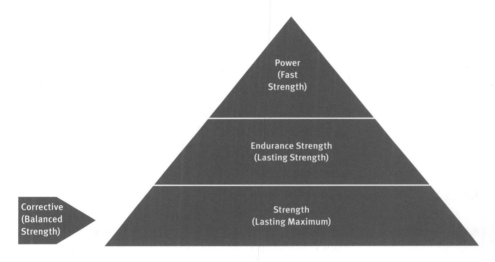

Figure 7: Functional Strength Training Phases

Strength Phase for Building Maximum Strength

The Strength Phase should be done in the pre-season to lay the foundation for better race performances later. During this phase, you will improve the ability of the core musculature to stabilize the pelvis and spine under heavier loads through the complete range of motion. The exercises will be difficult so you will only be able to do a few repetitions, but they will increase the load-bearing capabilities of your muscles, tendons, ligaments, and joints.

This phase is particularly important for ultra triathlon distance preparation because prolonged endurance training reduces lean body mass. Having some "extra" muscle (relatively speaking) will help you retain adequate lean body mass throughout your training. Strength lays the "brick and mortar" for the next phase of FST — muscular endurance.

Endurance Phase for Lasting Strength

The Endurance Phase builds endurance strength (lasting strength). The loads will be lighter than in the maximum strength phase so you will be able to perform more repetitions, usually three to four sets of 12 to 15 repetitions. Sometimes exercises are time-based, such as *"three sets of as many repetitions as you can do in 30 seconds."* This requires you to pace yourself.

Since the endurance strength phase utilizes a relatively light load, the musculature will improve its long slow contractile abilities without enlarging.

Power Phase for Fast Strength

When triathletes talk about power, it is usually in connection to power meters and cycling. But the concept of power applies to all three disciplines and being able to measure it isn't nearly as important as training to maximize it.

The power phase applies the gains from the earlier phases to the speeds and forces that the body will encounter on race day.

A solid strength base is needed in order to begin power training because maximum strength is important at the very beginning of the exercises to get the weight (or the body) moving. The greater the athlete's strength, the faster this initial motion will be. Less force and more speed are then required to continue and finish the movement.

The power phase focuses on moving against resistance quickly, just like you do when you swim, bike and run. In this phase, you will be doing fewer repetitions than in the previous phases.

Plyometrics

Plyometrics are explosive movements used in the power phase. The goal is to accelerate and project the resistance (which might be your own body) as far as possible.

Plyometric movements begin and end with the body in contact with something else — usually, but not always, the ground. These are typically jumps and hops that can be done with the legs or arms. Let's use a jump as an example: the leg muscles extend and lengthen, propelling you into space but then they must hold you (and any weight you are carrying) steady (resist shortening) to keep you from crumpling to the ground when you land. Notably, it is this holding steady (known as eccentric contraction) that causes the greatest muscle soreness (Friden, et. al. 1984).

Start with the easier moves and progress gradually to the more challenging ones. Plyometrics are identified in the power phase of the Sample Training Plan in Chapter 4.

Time Off

Recovery weeks are mandatory for endurance training, but not for strength training. When you skip your strength training for a week, you will be extra sore when you resume. If you feel very fatigued and want a break, compromise and do only one strength session during your recovery week. This is enough to keep the neuromuscular pathways alert.

When racing season is over, you need some recovery time to allow your mind and body to heal from the rigors of training and racing. You should take a break from your strength training, too. At some point, you will be ready to plan your next racing season and then the cycle of training will begin again.

Once you learn about your areas of weakness and have spent a season correcting them, you may feel that by taking time off you will lose what you have gained. Not so. The improvements to your neuromuscular system will not disintegrate in a month or two. When you return, you will get fit faster than before. Enjoy other activities to refresh your body and mind so you are ready for the next season.

Chapter 4
Sample FST
Exercise Program

This sample program is suitable for most triathletes. It is organized into the FST phases. Some of the exercises may seem too easy and some of them will be next to impossible. Follow the instructions to modify the difficulty of each exercise. The next chapter explains how to customize this program to suit your needs.

Form is important. It is harder to do the exercises correctly than it is to do them wrong. This program has exercises that can be done in 30-45 minutes depending upon the training phase. Always begin with the warm-up sequence.

Strength Training Warm-up

Angels
Lie face-up with the roller along and under your spine, head resting on the roller, knees bent, feet on the floor. Slide one arm to the side along the floor from your hip to above your head and back to your hip again, as if you are making a snow angel. Alternate arms.

Photo 15: Angels Start

Photo 16: Angels Finish

Backstroke
Lie face-up with the roller along and under your spine, head resting on the roller, knees bent, feet on the floor. Lift each arm off the floor one at a time. Move your arm from your hip to above your head, as if you are doing the backstroke.

Photo 17: Backstroke Start

Photo 18: Backstroke Finish

These two movements, calf roll-outs and IT band roll-outs are also used for self-myofascial release as discussed in Chapter 1.

Photo 19: Calf Roll-outs   *Photo 20: IT Band Roll-Outs*

Calf Roll-outs

With the foam roller perpendicular to your body, place one calf over the roller. Cross the other foot over, crossing your feet at the ankles. With your hands on the floor near your hips, push off the floor slightly and roll your calves over the roller.

IT Band Roll-outs

Place the foam roller perpendicular to your body, rest one thigh on the roller. Try to keep the thigh relaxed throughout the movement. Place your hands on the floor near your hips. Twist to the side, resting on the roller. With your hands, roll the side of your thigh up and down the roller from your knee to your hip. Switch sides.

Corrective Exercises

The first step is to correct any underlying problem that may rear its ugly head at some point down the road. These exercises correct basic flaws you have identified in the Functional Strength Assessment in Appendix A. They also provide a foundation to build upon during the Strength, Endurance Strength, and Power phases.

You should spend at least three weeks in the corrective phase then reassess your core strength (using the Functional Strength Assessment) again. If you fail that portion of the assessment, you should continue with the corrective phase for another three weeks because you need adequate core stability to begin the Strength Phase.

Start the Corrective phase with one set of 15 repetitions. Add a set in the second week and a third set in the third week. If you stay in this phase longer than three weeks, stick with three sets of 15 repetitions and adjust the exercises to make them more difficult.

Swiss Ball Y
Lay face down on a Swiss ball. The ball should be under your chest, with your hands on the floor in front of you. Extend your arms and lift them up forming a "Y" with your body and arms.

- Areas targeted: Lower trapezius (traps, upper back), shoulder blade stabilizers.
- Increase the difficulty by holding a dumbbell in each hand.
- Make the exercise easier by reducing the weight or doing the exercise one side at a time.
- You should feel the muscles on the bottom of your shoulder blades.
- Focus Point: Pull your shoulder blade into your "back pocket."

Photo 21: Swiss Ball Y

Swiss Ball T

Lay face down on a Swiss Ball. The ball should be under your chest, with your hands on the floor in front of you. Extend your arms to the side and lift them up forming a "T" with your body and arms.

- Areas targeted: Middle traps, rhomboids (between shoulder blades), and shoulder blade stabilizers.
- Increase the difficulty by holding a dumbbell in each hand.
- Make the exercise easier by reducing the weight or doing the exercise one side at a time.
- You should feel the muscles between your shoulder blades and behind your shoulders.
- Focus Point: Squeeze your shoulder blades.

Photo 22: Swiss Ball T

Swiss Ball W

Lay face down on a Swiss ball. The ball should be under your chest, with your hands on the floor in front of you. Bend your elbows and lift your arms to form a "W."

- Areas targeted: Rhomboids, upper traps, shoulder blade stabilizers.
- Increase the difficulty by holding a dumbbell in each hand.
- Make the exercise easier by reducing the weight or doing the exercise one side at a time.
- You should feel the muscles between your shoulder blades.
- Focus Point: Squeeze your shoulder blades.

Photo 23: Swiss Ball W

Standing Marbles

Scatter small pebbles or marbles on the floor in front of you. Place a cup or bowl about 12 inches in front and 12 inches to the outside of your support leg. Pick up as many marbles as you can with your toes while standing on the support leg and place them in the bowl.

- Areas targeted: Feet, ankles, hips, and gluteus maximus (glutes).
- Increase the difficulty by adding a resistance band around your waist. The band should be anchored to a wall at waist level and you should stand far enough away that you have to resist the pull of the band as you do the exercise.
- Make the exercise easier by holding on to a chair with one hand.
- You should feel the muscles on the bottom of feet, calves, and glutes.
- Focus Point: Imagine balancing on a tripod between the ball of your foot — big toe, little toe and heel.

Photo 24: Standing Marbles

Swiss Ball Bridge

Begin lying on your back with your feet on the ball, knees bent. Raise your body into a bridge position, lower and repeat.

- Areas targeted: Glutes and hamstrings (back of thigh).
- Increase the difficulty by bending your knees more.
- Make the exercise easier by straightening your knees.
- You should feel the muscles in your glutes and hamstrings.
- Focus Point: Drive your hips toward the ceiling.

Photo 25: Swiss Ball Bridge

Swiss Ball Push- up

Get into a push-up position with the ball under your feet. Keep your body line straight and lower your chin to the ground, then back up again.

- Areas targeted: Chest, abs, and triceps.
- Increase the difficulty by moving farther out on the ball.
- Make the exercise easier by moving the ball closer to your knees.
- You should feel the muscles in your chest, in front of your shoulders, and in the abs and triceps.
- Focus Point: Maintain a straight body. Don't let your hips sag.

Photo 26: Swiss Ball Push-up

Swiss Ball Plank

Start with your knees on the floor and elbows resting on the ball. Clasp your hands together. Lift your hips into a plank position and hold. Make sure to keep your back straight throughout the motion.

- Area targeted: Abs.
- Increase the difficulty by rolling the ball out.
- Make the exercise easier by starting on your knees.
- You should feel the muscles in your abs.
- Focus Point: Don't let your hips sag.

Photo 27: Swiss Ball Plank

Swiss Ball Side Plank

Lie sideways on a mat, resting on one elbow. Place a Swiss ball between your knees and squeeze. Lift your body off the floor and hold.

- Areas targeted: Obliques, abs, and hip adductors (move leg toward the body).
- Increase the difficulty by moving your elbow out.
- Make the exercise easier by removing the ball and bending your knees.
- You should feel the muscles in your hips and core.
- Focus Point: Keep your body straight. Don't let your hips fall back.

Photo 28: Swiss Ball Side Plank

Strength Exercises

The strength phase provides a foundation that the Endurance and Power phases will build upon. It should be difficult to complete eight to 10 repetitions of each exercise. Attempt to complete three or four sets. Spend six to eight weeks in this phase.

Hamstring Trio

Part 1: Bridge — Begin by lying on your back with feet on the ball, knees bent. Raise your body into a bridge position, lower and repeat.

Part 2: March — Begin by lying on your back with feet on the ball, knees bent. Raise your body into a bridge position, hold and lift your foot a few inches off the ball. Return to the ball and lift the opposite foot. Maintain the bridge position throughout the set.

Part 3: Hamstring curl — Begin by lying on your back with feet on the ball. Raise your body into a bridge position. Bend knees and bring feet toward body, rolling the ball toward you. Return to starting position. Repeat.

- Areas targeted: Glutes and hamstrings.
- Increase the difficulty by bending your knees more and lifting your hands off the ground.
- Make the exercise easier by straightening your knees.
- You should feel the muscles in your glutes and hamstrings.
- Focus Point: Try to maintain a level pelvis on all motions.

Photo 29: Hamstring Trio Start

Photo 30: Hamstring Trio Bridge

Photo 31: Hamstring Trio March

Photo 32: Hamstring Trio Curl

TRX Reverse Lunge

Stand facing the TRX with arms extended, slightly bent, at shoulder height. Hold the handles and create some tension in the straps. Drive one foot back as you push your hips back and lower your body by bending the knee. Keep your back leg as straight as possible while keeping your foot off the ground. Pause, then return to the starting position.

- Areas targeted: Glutes, hamstrings, quads, and calves.
- Increase the difficulty by starting farther away from the TRX anchor.
- Make the exercise easier by straightening your knees.
- You should feel the muscles in your glutes and hamstrings.
- Focus Point: Drive your back leg back but don't let it rest on the ground.

Photo 33: TRX Reverse Lunge

Triplanar Calf Raise

This calf raise is a sequence of three positions. Stand on a raised block or other step about 2" tall. Stand on the step and let the other foot hang freely. Raise your body from the calf, bringing the other knee up to hip level straight in front of you. Return to starting position. Next, raise the same knee in front of you then move it across your body toward the opposite hip and return to the starting position. Now bring the knee up and move it to the side away from your body. Return to the starting position.

- Area targeted: Calves.
- Increase the difficulty by holding a dumbbell in each hand.
- Make the exercise easier by eliminating the step and holding onto something for balance.
- You should feel the muscles in your calves.
- Focus Point: Don't start with too many! Your calves will be very sore the next day if you do.

Photo 34: Triplaner Calf Raise Start

Photo 35: Triplanar Calf
Raise External

Photo 36: Triplanar Calf
Raise Internal

Photo 37: Triplantar Calf Raise Forward

Scorpion on Swiss Ball

Lay on your stomach on the ball and roll forward until your hands reach the floor in front of you. Walk your hands out until your shins rest on top of the ball. Lift your knee off the ball and toward your opposite shoulder. Drive your foot back up and rotate your entire lower body, lifting your foot toward the ceiling.

- Area targeted: Abs.
- Increase the difficulty by moving the ball closer to your toes.
- Make the exercise easier by moving the ball closer to your knees.
- You should feel the muscles in your abs.
- Focus Point: You should only feel this in your abs. If you feel it in your lower back, move the ball closer to your knees.

Photo 38: Scorpion on Swiss Ball Start

Photo: 39: Scorpion on Swiss Ball Rotate

TRX Plank

Feet in TRX; elbows on ground, hold body in plank position.

• Area targeted: Abs.
• Increase the difficulty by moving away from the TRX anchor.
• Make the exercise easier by starting closer to the TRX anchor or eliminate the TRX altogether.
• You should feel the muscles in your abs.
• Focus Point: Don't let your hips drop. Maintain a straight body line.

Photo 40: TRX Plank

Swiss Ball Rows

Begin by balancing on your knees on a Swiss ball. Using a sport cord/resistance band or pulley, pull your arms back as you bend your elbows. Initiate the pull with the back and draw your shoulder blades in close together without shrugging your shoulders

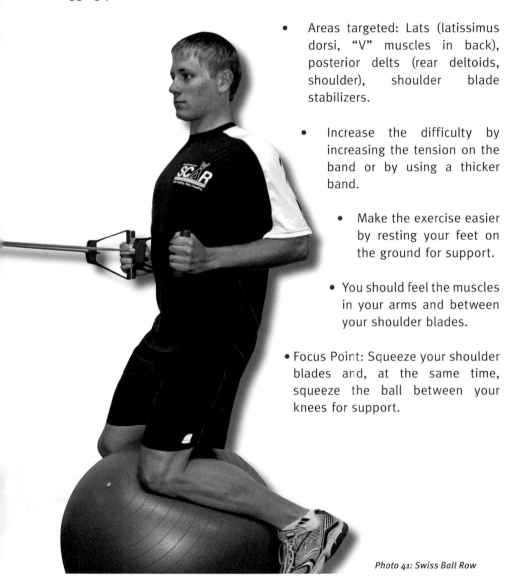

- Areas targeted: Lats (latissimus dorsi, "V" muscles in back), posterior delts (rear deltoids, shoulder), shoulder blade stabilizers.

- Increase the difficulty by increasing the tension on the band or by using a thicker band.

- Make the exercise easier by resting your feet on the ground for support.

- You should feel the muscles in your arms and between your shoulder blades.

- Focus Point: Squeeze your shoulder blades and, at the same time, squeeze the ball between your knees for support.

Photo 41: Swiss Ball Row

TRX Matrix

Face the TRX with your arms extended straight in front of you at shoulder height as if you were firing a pistol. There should be some tension on the straps and you should hold onto them both with one hand. Your feet should be facing straight forward. Reach back with your free hand as you rotate your body in the same direction. Pull the shoulder blades together as you rotate up and reach back with your free hand. Your trunk should go through a 180° arc. Return to the open position and repeat.

- Areas targeted: Biceps, shoulder blade stabilizers, core rotation.
- Increase the difficulty by starting with your feet closer to the wall/anchor and holding a weight in your hand.
- Make the exercise easier by starting with your feet farther away from the wall/anchor.
- You should feel the muscles in your abs.
- Focus Point: Pull your shoulder blades back.

Photo 42: TRX Matrix Start

Photo 43: TRX Matrix Finish

Swiss Ball Chest Press

Lay on your back over a Swiss ball. The ball should be under your shoulder blades. Keep your hips extended and press the dumbbells up. Return to the starting position. Repeat

- Areas targeted: Chest, shoulders, and arms.
- Increase the difficulty by increasing the weight of the dumbbells.
- Make the exercise easier by moving the ball closer to your knees.
- You should feel the muscles in your abs.
- Focus Point: Keep your hips up and level.

Photo 44: Swiss Ball Chest Press

Resistance Band/Cable Chops (up and down)

To chop down, anchor the resistance band above shoulder height. Clasp both hands around the resistance band handles and step away so that your side and shoulder face the anchor point. In one movement, while keeping your arms straight, rotate your torso down and across your body so your hands end up outside your opposite hip. Pause, then return to the starting position.

To chop up, anchor the resistance band below knee level. This time, start with the hands low and rotate your torso while bringing the hands up across your body. Your hands should end up above your head outside your opposite shoulder.

- Areas targeted: Shoulder blade stabilizers and core rotation.
- Increase the difficulty by standing in a lunge position. The leg nearest the anchor should be forward.
- Make the exercise easier by standing with your feet shoulder width apart.
- You should feel the muscles in your abs and arms.
- Focus Point: Initiate the motion with a pull and finish with a push.

Photo 45: Resistance Band/Cable Chops Down Photo

Photo 46: Resistance Band/Cable Chops Up

Endurance Strength Exercises

The Endurance Strength phase will help you apply strength over the long haul. You can start by doing these exercises as a circuit with one set of each exercise as one round. Start with doing as many reps as you can in 30 seconds. Take a minimal amount of rest between exercises. Increase the time by five seconds per week until you get to 60 seconds per exercise. You can do more than one set of each exercise or add more rounds as you progress.

TRX Back Rotation Lunge (Cross Lunge)

Stand facing the TRX, holding on with arms extended, slightly bent, at shoulder height. There should be some tension in the straps. Step backward with your one leg crossing behind the other. Lower your body until your support knee is bent at least 90 degrees. Return to the starting position and repeat.

- Areas targeted: Core and hips.
- Increase the difficulty by moving your feet closer to the TRX anchor.
- Make the exercise easier by moving your feet away from the TRX anchor.
- You should feel the muscles in your core, spine extensors, glutes and hamstrings.
- Focus Point: Don't let your back foot hit the ground.

Photo 47: TRX Back Rotation Lunge (Cross Lunge)

TRX Plank Saws

Get into a plank position with both feet in the TRX and elbows on the ground. Hold the body in a plank position and slide your body away from your elbows toward the anchor like your body is a saw. Return to the start position and repeat.

- Area targeted: Core.
- Increase the difficulty by moving your feet farther away from the TRX anchor/wall.
- Make the exercise easier by moving your feet closer to the anchor/wall.
- You should feel the muscles in your abs.
- Focus Point: Keep your hips up.

Photo 48: TRX Plank Saws

TRX Atomic Push-ups

Place both feet in the foot cradles of a TRX. Get into push-up position. Perform a push-up by lowering your body until your chest is just above the floor and then pressing back up. Bring your knees toward your elbows in a crunching movement. Pause and return to the starting position.

- Areas targeted: Core, chest, and shoulders.
- Increase the difficulty by moving your feet away from the TRX anchor.
- Make the exercise easier by moving your feet closer to the TRX anchor.
- You should feel the muscles in your abs, pecs, and shoulders.
- Focus Point: Lift your hips toward the ceiling.

Photo 49: TRX Atomic Push-ups

TRX Rows

Stand facing the TRX with a handle in each hand and back away until you feel tension in the straps. Keep your body straight but at a steep angle and initiate the pull with the back, not the arms. Draw your shoulder blades in close together without shrugging the shoulders.

- Areas targeted: Back and shoulders.
- Increase the difficulty by moving your feet closer to the TRX anchor.
- Make the exercise easier by moving your feet away from the TRX anchor.
- You should feel the muscles in your back and shoulders.
- Focus Point: Combine the motion with a squat to maximize the benefit.

Photo 50: TRX Rows

TRX Y.I.W.

Stand facing the TRX with a handle in each hand and back away until you feel tension in the straps. Your body should form a 45- to 60-degree angle to the floor, and your arms should be parallel to the floor. Pull your body toward the anchor point by pulling your hands up and over your head while squeezing your shoulders together. When your arms are extended out, your body and arms should form an "I." Return to the starting position then pull your body toward the anchor point again, this time lifting your arms up and apart, forming a "Y." Repeat, this time bending the elbows so your arms form a "W." Go back to the starting position after each letter.

- Area targeted: Shoulders.
- Increase the difficulty by moving your feet closer to the TRX anchor.
- Make the exercise easier by moving your feet away from the TRX anchor.
- You should feel the muscles in your back and shoulders.
- Focus Point: Keep your hands up and elbows straight through the entire movement.

Photo 50: TRX Y

Photo 51: TRX I

Photo 52: TRX W

TRX Chest Press

Stand with your back to the TRX, one hand in each loop. Lean forward and extend the arms in front of your body. Keep a straight body line with by contracting the glutes and keeping your shoulders pulled down and back. Bend the elbows and allow the body to tilt forward then press your body back to the starting position. Keep the hands high enough to prevent the straps from rubbing arms during the exercise. Repeat.

- Areas targeted: Chest and abs.
- Increase the difficulty by moving your feet closer to the TRX anchor and/or lifting one foot off the ground.
- Make the exercise easier by moving your feet away from the TRX anchor.
- You should feel the muscles in your abs and pecs (pectorals, chest) and deltoids.
- Focus Point: Keep your back straight.

Photo 52: TRX Chest Press Start

Photo 53: TRX Chest Press Push

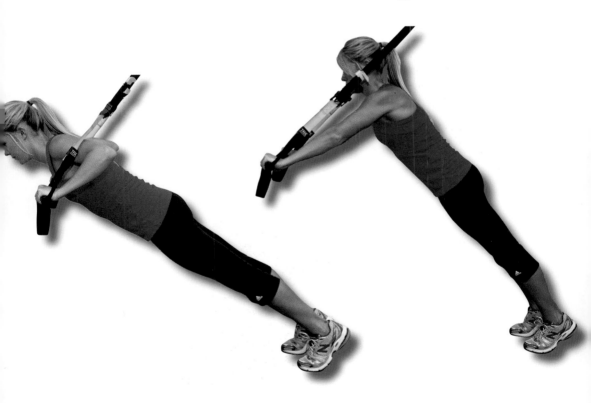

TRX Triceps Press

Stand facing away from the TRX with a handle in each hand and tension in the straps. Keep elbows bent, shoulder width apart and pointing straight ahead. Straighten the elbows and press your body into a more upright position. Return to the starting position. Repeat.

- Area targeted: Arms.
- Increase the difficulty by moving your feet closer to the TRX anchor and/or lifting one foot off the ground.
- Make the exercise easier by moving your feet away from the TRX anchor.
- You should feel the muscles in your triceps.
- Focus Point: Keep your body straight (stable core) through the motion.

Photo 56: TRX Triceps Press

TRX Bicep Curl

Stand facing the TRX with a strap in each hand and tension in the straps. Your body should form a 45-to 60-degree angle to the floor, and your arms should be straight with your palms up. Without moving your upper arms, bend your elbows and curl the handles toward your shoulder, your palms facing your forehead. Pause and return to the starting position.

- Area targeted: Arms.
- Increase the difficulty by moving your feet closer to the TRX anchor and/or lifting one foot off the ground.
- Make the exercise easier by moving your feet away from the TRX anchor.
- You should feel the muscles in your biceps.
- Focus Point: Keep your body straight (stable core) through the motion.

Photo 57: TRX Bicep Curl Start   *Photo 58: TRX Bicep Curl Pull*

TRX Side Step Lunge

Stand facing the TRX with arms extended, holding a loop in each hand. Arms should be slightly bent, at shoulder height. Stand far enough from the anchor that there is tension on the loops. Take a big step to your side as you push your hips backward and lower your body by dropping your hips and bending your knee, keeping tension in the loops. When you step to the right, bend your right knee. Your opposite leg should remain straight. Pause, then return to the starting position.

- Areas targeted: Hips and knees.
- Increase the difficulty by moving your feet toward the wall.
- Make the exercise easier by your feet away from the wall.
- You should feel the muscles in your glutes, quads, calves, and hamstrings.
- Focus Point: Stay tall and keep your knee behind your toe.

Photo 59: Side Step Lunge

TRX Reverse (suspended) Lunges

Stand facing away from the TRX anchor. Balance on one foot and place the other foot into the foot cradles. Stand such that the support leg is straight and the suspended foot is behind you (similar to a running stance). Lower your body as you move the suspended leg back into a lunge position until your back (suspended) knee almost touches the floor and your support leg is bent 90 degrees. Press through the heel of your support leg to stand back up. Repeat.

- Areas targeted: Hips and knees.
- Increase the difficulty by moving your feet away from the wall.
- Make the exercise easier by moving your feet closer to the wall.
- You should feel the muscles in your glutes, quads, calves, and hamstrings.
- Focus Point: Stay tall and keep your knee behind your toe.

Photo 60: Reverse (Suspended) Lunges

TRX Side Plank Rotations

Put both of your feet in the TRX loops while supporting yourself with one elbow on the ground as your body is in the side plank position. Extend the other arm straight up so it is perpendicular to your body. Now rotate your hips forward while reaching down and underneath with your free hand. Return to the starting position, reaching up toward the ceiling.

- Areas targeted: Shoulders, core, and hips.
- Increase the difficulty by moving your feet away from the wall/anchor and holding a weight in your hand.
- Make the exercise easier by moving closer to the wall/anchor.
- You should feel the muscles in your abs.
- Focus Point: Keep your hips up and your body in line with your legs.

Photo 61: TRX Side Plank Rotations Start

Photo 62: TRX Side Plank Rotations Move

Side Steps

Place a resistance band around your ankles. Side step while keeping your toes forward. Continue for 30 seconds, then switch direction.

- Area targeted: Hip abductors (move leg away from body).
- Increase the difficulty by taking larger steps and/or using a band with greater resistance.
- Make the exercise easier by using a band with less resistance.
- You should feel the muscles in your glutes.
- Focus Point: Keep your toes straight ahead.

Photo 63: Side Steps

Cone Reach

Set up three cones in the shape of a triangle in front of you. Stand on one foot. Lower your upper body and reach the opposite hand to a cone. Hinge from your hips and keep your back straight. Extend your back leg behind you as you reach. Return to the starting position and continue to reach for the other two cones.

- Areas targeted: Feet, hips, knees and ankles.
- Increase the difficulty by moving your feet away from the cones.
- Make the exercise easier by reaching toward taller cones.
- You should feel the muscles in your hips, quads, and calves.
- Focus Point: Reach with the hand opposite your support leg.

Photo 64: Cone Reach

Power Exercises

Now that you are good and strong, you will work on moving weight around with greater speed. The movements in this phase should be done quickly, explosively if you can. You need to apply the most force at the very beginning of the exercise to get things moving. Work toward three sets of eight to 10 repetitions.

Medicine Ball Cones

Set up three cones in the shape of a triangle in front of you as done previously. Stand on one foot. Hold a medicine ball and hinge from your hips while keeping your back straight. Lower your upper body toward the ground and reach the ball toward the first cone as your back leg extends behind you. Return to the starting position and continue to reach for the other two cones.

- Areas targeted: Feet, hips, knees, and ankles.
- Increase the difficulty by moving your feet away from the cones and increasing the weight of the ball.
- Make the exercise easier by reaching toward taller cones.
- You should feel the muscles in your hips, quads, calves, and shoulders.
- Focus Point: Keep your back flat as you reach.

Photo 65: Medicine Ball Cones

TRX SL Reverse (suspended) Lunge Hop (plyometrics)

Stand facing away from the TRX anchor. Balance on one foot and place the other foot into the foot cradles. Stand so that the support leg is straight and the suspended foot is behind you (similar to a running stance). Lower your body as you move the suspended leg back into a lunge position until your back (suspended) knee almost touches the floor and your support leg is bent 90 degrees. As you press through your left heel to stand back up, drive your hands up and hop off the ground. Perform all your repetitions and then repeat with the other leg.

- Areas targeted: Hips, knees, and ankles.
- Increase the difficulty by moving your feet away from wall.
- Make the exercise easier by moving toward the wall.
- You should feel the muscles in your hips, quads, and calves.
- Focus Point: Drive your arm up as you hop.

Photo 66: TRX SL Reverse (Suspended) Lunge Hop

Photo 67: TRX SL Reverse (Suspended) Lunge Hop Back

Medicine Ball Squat Jump (Plyometrics)

Start in a squatting position with a medicine ball on the ground in front of you. Lift the ball quickly overhead as you jump with both feet. Bring the ball back down, let it touch the ground, and then repeat the jump.

- Areas targeted: Hips, knees and ankles, shoulders, core.
- Increase the difficulty by moving your feet away from the cones.
- Make the exercise easier by reaching toward taller cones.
- You should feel the muscles in your hips, quads, calves, and shoulders.
- Focus Point: Drive the ball up as you jump.

Photo 68: Medicine Ball Squat Jump Start

Photo 69: Medicine Ball Squat in Air

Skips (Plyometrics)

Just like when you were a kid: Skip 100 feet while driving your arms and opposite knee up.

- Areas targeted: Coordination and running form.
- Increase the difficulty by increasing the height of your skip.
- Make the exercise easier by slowing down and skipping lower.
- You should feel the muscles in your legs.
- Focus Point: Drive your arm up.

Photo 70: Skips

Bosu Push-up (Plyometrics)

Position a Bosu®Balance Trainer, dome side up, on the floor. Place your hands on the Bosu. Lift one hand off the ball and put on the ground. Complete one push (one hand on the ground, the other on the Bosu) but drive forcefully back up you so you can quickly return your hand to the Bosu. Repeat with the other hand.

- Areas targeted: Chest and abs.
- Increase the difficulty by moving faster.
- Make the exercise easier by slowing down.
- You should feel the muscles in your abs, pecs, and deltoids.
- Focus Point: Keep your back straight.

Photo 71: Bosu Push-up Start

to 72: Bosu Push-up Floor

Photo 73: Bosu Push-up End

Side Step Cones (Plyometrics)

Set up two cones approximately 8-10 feet apart. Place a light resistance band around your ankles. Facing the cones, take a step toward a cone and reach down, touching it with your opposite hand. Immediately spring back to the other foot then reach for the other cone with your other hand. Repeat quickly, side to side.

- Areas targeted: Hips, knees, and ankles.
- Increase the difficulty by moving the cones farther apart.
- Make the exercise easier by slowing down and moving the cones closer.
- You should feel the muscles in your hips, quads, and calves.
- Focus Point: Reach across your body to the cone.

Photo 74: Side Step Cones

Medicine Ball Throws (Plyometrics)

Begin on your back, shoulder blades resting on the ball. Knees should be at a 90° angle. Use an overhead motion to throw a medicine ball to a partner. Your partner will then throw the ball back to you. Catch it while bringing it over your head and toward the floor.

- Areas targeted: Core and shoulders.
- Increase the difficulty by moving your feet closer together.
- Make the exercise easier with a lighter medicine ball.
- You should feel the muscles in your abs.
- Focus Point: Bring the ball as far as you can over your head.

Photo 75: Medicine Ball Throws

Photo 76: Medicine Ball Throws Catch

Bent over Freestyle Pull (resistance band/cable)

Stand with your knees slightly bent. Bend forward at the hip until your body is parallel to the ground. One hand should be forward in the maximum reach position, like when you swim. There should be some tension on the resistance band. Pull the lead hand back following the same pattern as a freestyle stroke. Recover with high elbow and repeat.

- Areas targeted: Shoulders and core, specific for swimming.
- Increase the difficulty by using a stronger band.
- Make the exercise easier by lowering the resistance or moving closer to the wall.
- Focus Point: Keep your back flat and elbow high. Follow your freestyle (pull) motion.

Photo 77: Bent Over Freestyle Pull Start

Photo 78: Bent Over Freestyle Pull Middle

Photo 79: Bent Over Freestyle Pull Finish

TRX Pendulum Swings

Begin with your feet in the TRX loops and get into push-up position. Rotate your hips to the right and then back to the left. Get into a swinging motion. Attempt to stop your momentum on every third swing so you alternate sides.

- Areas targeted: Chest, shoulders and abdominals
- Increase the difficulty by increasing the speed and swing
- Make the exercise easier by slowing down.
- You should feel the muscles in your abs, pecs, and deltoids
- Focus Point: Keep your back straight. It will be difficult to actually stop the motion at the apex but the attempt will stimulate your nervous system.

Photo 80: TRX Pendulum Swings

Chapter 5
Customize Your FST Plan

Now that you have seen what the exercises look like, you need to fit the various FST phases into your existing endurance training plan. These simple steps will help you customize your FST program:

Step 1: Schedule the training phases
Step 2: Choose the exercises and adjust difficulty as needed
Step 3: Work FST into your training schedule

Step 1: Schedule the training phases

Your plan should include all of the functional strength training phases in the order set forth in Figure 8.

Phase	1	2	3	4
	Corrective (Balanced Strength)	Stabilization (Maximum Strength)	Endurance (Lasting Strength)	Power (Fast Strength)

Figure 8: Functional Strength Training Phase Progression

If you already have a periodized training plan for endurance work, you can add strength training to the existing training phases. Figure 11 shows where the FST phases fit into two popular training models.

Model	Training Phases						
Bompa	Preparation			Competitive			Transition
Friel	Preparation	Base	Build	Peak	Race		Recovery
FST	Balanced Strength	Maximum Strength	Endurance Strength	Fast Strength			Rest

Figure 9: How functional strength training fits in with other training models

The adaptations stimulated by FST are both muscular (changes in muscle size and composition) and neuromuscular (enhanced two-way communication between the brain and the musculoskeletal system). It takes about six weeks for your muscles to adapt to a strength routine but the neuromuscular changes occur more quickly, usually in about two weeks. Each phase is beneficial even if it is shorter than six weeks.

If you can devote six weeks to each phase, terrific. If not, you will have to adjust the amount of time you spend in each of the phases. Each phase is important, but some are more crucial than others.

Here are the guidelines:
- The Corrective Phase is necessary as it "wakes up" your core. You should spend a minimum of three weeks in this phase.

- The Endurance Strength Phase is second priority (although it is the third phase). If time is very short, you can get by with just three weeks of corrective work and spend the rest of the time working on endurance strength.

- The Stabilization Phase is the second phase but the third priority. It is especially important for those who have been sedentary for several years and women. It is also very important for ultra triathlon distance racers. If you are in one of these categories, spend at least three weeks in this phase.

- The Power Phase is the lowest priority, and it is also the final phase. It is mandatory for podium chasers in any distance and off-road enthusiasts, and it is icing on the cake for ultra triathlon distance athletes. Since benefits come quickly, even a few sessions are worth doing if you can.

Step 2: Choose the Exercises and Adjust Difficulty as Needed

The sample FST program in Chapter 4 has a selection of exercises that are suitable for most triathletes. Start with those and adjust the difficulty if needed.

The Functional Strength Training Model in Figure 10 shows what the various training phases look like in terms of intensity. Rather than changing the amount of weight used in the various phases, FST defines intensity by the difficulty of the exercises. So if you can only do three sets of eight, that exercise is suitable for the Maximum Strength Phase. By modifying an exercise in such a way that you can do three sets of 15, that exrcise can be done in the Endurance Phase and so on.

The level of difficulty is determined by the type and complexity of the movements, adding stability and balance challenges, and the use of various forms of resistance like weighted balls, resistance bands and similar apparatus.

FST Phase	Corrective	Stabilization	Endurance	Power
Volume	Depends upon area of weakness	Work up to 3 sets of 8 repetitions	Work up to 3 sets of 15-20 repetitions (or 3 sets of 30 seconds) with minimal rest	Work up to 3-5 sets of 2-4 repetitions done explosively
Intensity	Adjusted so athlete can perform the movement correctly without compensating	Adjusted so athlete can perform the volume of movements correctly without compensating	Adjusted so athlete can perform the volume of movements correctly without compensating	Plyometrics or speed-based movements
Example using a push-up exercise	Rehabilitate shoulder or core problems that prevent athlete from being able to do a push-up with proper form and without pain	Push-ups with hands on a Bosu™ Balance Trainer, modified as needed so athlete can barely do 3-4 sets of 8	Push-ups with feet perched in a TRX suspension trainer so athlete can barely do 3 sets of 15.	Push-ups done with enough momentum to allow a handclap between each. Athlete can only do a few of these.

Figure 10: Functional Strength Training Model

You should replace the exercises with new ones after six weeks, even if you remain in the same training phase. Changing the exercises is important because you want to keep your neuromuscular system guessing to maximize adaptation. Most of the exercises can be done in any training phase as you can see in Figure 11. Remember, it is the intensity of the exercise (level of difficulty, number of sets and repetitions) that determines which phase an exercise belongs in, not the movement itself. By altering the intensity of the exercise it can be used in any training phase. The exceptions are the plyometric exercises, which are only suitable for the Power Phase.

Exercise	Target (abbreviated)	Equipment*	Training Phase exercise is found in
Swiss Ball Y	Trapezius, shoulder blade stabilizers	Swiss ball	Corrective/Any
Swiss Ball T	Trapezius, rhomboids, and shoulder blade stabilizers	Swiss ball	Corrective/Any
Swiss Ball W	Rhomboids, upper traps, shoulder blade stabilizers	Swiss ball	Corrective/Any
Standing Marbles	Feet, ankles, hips and glutes	Standing Marbles	Corrective/Any
Swiss Ball Bridge	Glutes and hamstrings	Swiss ball	Corrective/Any

Exercise	Target (abbreviated)	Equipment*	Training Phase exercise is found in
Swiss Ball Push-up	Chest, abs, triceps	Swiss ball	Corrective/Any
Swiss Ball Plank	Abdominals	Swiss ball	Corrective/Any
Swiss Ball Side Plank	Obliques, abs, hip adductors	Swiss ball	Corrective/Any
Hamstring Trio	Glutes and hamstrings	Swiss ball	Strength/Any
TRX Reverse Lunge	Glutes, hamstrings, quads, and calves	TRX	Strength/Any
Triplanar Calf Raise	Calves	Step	Strength/Any
Scorpion on Swiss Ball	Abdominals	Swiss ball	Strength/Any
TRX Plank	Abdominals	TRX	Strength/Any
Swiss Ball Row	Lats, posterior deltoids, shoulder blade stabilizers	Swiss ball, resistance band**	Strength/Any
TRX Matrix	Biceps, shoulder blade stabilizers, core rotation	TRX	Strength/Any
Swiss Ball Chest Press	Chest, shoulders, arms	Swiss ball, dumbbells	Strength/Any
Resistance Band/Cable Chops (up and down)	Shoulder blade stabilizers, core rotation	Resistance band/ cable	Strength/Any
TRX Back Rotation Lunge (cross lunge)	Core, hips	TRX	Endurance Strength/Any
TRX Plank Saws	Core	TRX	Endurance Strength/Any
TRX Atomic Push-ups	Core, chest, shoulders	TRX	Endurance Strength/Any
TRX Rows	Back, shoulders	TRX	Endurance Strength/Any
TRX Y.I.W.	Shoulders and rotator cuff	TRX	Endurance Strength/Any
TRX Chest Press	Chest, abdominals	TRX	Endurance Strength/Any
TRX Triceps Press	Arms	TRX	Endurance Strength/Any
TRX Bicep Curl	Arms	TRX	Endurance Strength/Any
TRX Side Step Lunge	Hips, knees	TRX	Endurance Strength/Any
TRX Reverse (suspended) Lunges	Hips, knees	TRX	Endurance Strength/Any

Exercise	Target (abbreviated)	Equipment*	Training Phase exercise is found in
TRX Side Plank Rotations	Shoulders, core, hips	TRX	Endurance Strength/Any
Side Steps	Hip abductors	Resistance band	Endurance Strength/Any
Cone Reach	Feet, hips, knees, ankles	Cones***	Endurance Strength/Any
Medicine Ball Cones	Feet, hips, knees, ankles	Medicine ball, Cones	Power
TRX SL Reverse (suspended) Lunge Hop	Hips, knees, ankles	TRX	Power
Medicine Ball Squat Jump	Hips, knees, ankles, shoulders, core	Medicine ball	Power
Skips	Coordination and running form		Power
Bosu Push-up	Chest, abdominals	Bosu® Balance Trainer	Power
Side Step Cones	Hips, knees, ankles	Resistance band, cones	Power
Medicine Ball Throws	Shoulders, core	Medicine ball	Power
Bent Over Freestyle Pull	Shoulders, core	Resistance band	Power/Any
TRX Pendulum Swings	Chest, shoulders, abdominals	TRX	Power

*Many of the exercises can be made more difficult by adding weights up to 20 lbs
**Resistance band, tubing, cables, and sport bands can be used interchangeably. ***Cones can be substituted with other objects.

Figure 11: Summary of FST Exercises in Sample Program

You will need the equipment specified in Figure 11. Equipment is discussed in detail in Chapter 6.

Adjust the Level of Difficulty

Here are some guidelines to keep in mind when manipulating the intensity of the exercises.

1. Develop technique on stable surfaces before progressing to unstable ones. Doing a push-up with your feet and hands on the floor is much easier than doing it when your feet are resting on a ball. The ball makes you wobble so you have to use your core muscles to provide stability and balance as you

do the movement. The Functional Strength Training Phases begin with more stable surfaces and progress to less stable ones. Likewise, most exercises can be adapted from one phase to another by manipulating the amount of instability, among other things. Thus, you can do push-ups on the floor in the Corrective Phase, then do them on a ball in the Strength phase, and so on.

2. Begin with body weight when practical. Sometimes body weight is too little and sometimes it is too much. Equipment like a Swiss ball or foam roller can make you less stable and thus make exercises harder, but they can also be used to add support, making an exercise easier. If regular push-ups are too difficult, put a Swiss ball under your thighs (so you lay on the ball) and proceed that way. As you get stronger, you will be able to move the ball farther down your legs. Difficulty increases as less of your bodyweight is supported by the ball.

3. The difficulty of a given exercise should be such that during the final set, you struggle mightily. You may not be able to complete it.

4. Once you have figured out which exercises to do and the amount of weight/ resistance to use, write it out on the blank workout card like the one in Figure 12.

Step 3: Work FST into Your Training Schedule

Most triathletes would rather spend their training hours swimming, biking and running than being in the gym. Two 30-45-minute sessions per week is plenty to reap the benefits of FST. There may be times when you spend more time in the gym to rehabilitate an injury or to build an extra strength base before a particularly challenging season but that should be the exception, not the rule.

The first time you do the exercises, it will take about 30% longer than it will once you get used to the exercises. Write out your planned exercises on a workout card like the one in Figure 12 or keep this book handy and mark the exercises you will do. Make notes about the modifications needed so you don't have to figure it out again during your next workout.

How to combine strength and aerobic training

Time in the gym does not have to add to total training time. An appropriate strength training program can be used as a substitute for up to 20% of weekly endurance training with no ill effects (Mikola 2007). That means you can spend a little less time pounding your legs on the pavement and improve performance at the same time by hitting the gym, or you can reduce your training time in each discipline by about 20 minutes per week to allow for 60 minutes in the gym.

Do endurance work first in any given training day. Research suggests that triathletes would benefit more from an endurance-strength brick (Chtara 2005) than doing the sessions separately or doing strength work first. Remember, a brick is doing the disciplines (usually bike to run) without rest between them. A British study examined how sequencing the order of endurance sessions and strength training sessions influenced a 4 km time trial running test. The subjects were college men who were not athletes. They did the time trial and other tests before and then after a 12-week program combining endurance and strength training in various sequences. At the end of the study, all of the subjects were faster but the ones who did the endurance-strength brick improved their speed 4% more than the group that did the strength-endurance brick. Swim in the gym's pool or finish your run or bike at the gym so you can go immediately into your strength work to get the maximum benefit.

Start Conservatively

You should expect to be very sore within 1-2 days of your first session. You may wish to take a more conservative approach and on the first day, perform only one set of each exercise. This will make you less sore. Do two sets the second session and work toward three sets after that. Don't strength train on consecutive days. You need the recovery days between sessions for the adaptations to take hold.

Exercise	Notes	Wt/Reps	Wt/Reps	Wt/Reps	Wt/Reps	Wt/Reps	Wt/Reps	Wt/Reps	Wt/Reps	Wt/Reps	Wt/Reps	Wt/Reps

Figure 12: Sample Blank Workout Card

Chapter 6
Equipment

Access to a gym is nice, but most gyms are full of useless weight machines. Most gyms don't have the equipment you will need. Check to see that the gym has what you need before you join. You can also equip your home with all that you need for a fraction of the cost. Refer to Figure 11 in Chapter 5 for a list of equipment that you need for each particular exercise.

Workspace

Sure, it is great to see yourself looking lean and strong as you do your FST, but a mirror lets you see if your hips are sagging or your foot is going off in the wrong direction when you do your exercises. You don't need a wall of mirrors, but a large, full-length mirror is a great help. You will also need some space. Don't do your exercises close to furniture. FST training requires balance, the maximum range of motion and considerable effort so create a safe and useful workspace. Wearing headphones will help you stay focused on what you are doing and discourage family members from interrupting you.

Exercise Mat

Carpets, rugs and hard flooring can make some of the exercises impossible. An exercise mat will keep you from getting rug burn and at the same time it will provide enough friction so you can hold your position. The surface of the mat should be comfortable against your skin. Get a foam or rubber mat that is relatively firm, not one that is so heavily padded that it creates instability. Brands include Airex™, Aeromat™ and GoFit™.

Equipment for Dynamic Warm-up and Self-myofascial Release

Foam Roller
Foam Rollers come in various lengths and levels of firmness. You will need a long one, about 35", to do your dynamic warm-up. Some of them are smooth and others are rough and require a cover to use for comfort against bare skin. A firm roller is the most versatile because it can be used both for self-myofascial release and as a surface to create instability for your strength exercises. Brands include EVA™, and PB Elite™.
Textured rollers like the the Grid Roller™ and Thera-Roll ™are very effective for self-myofascial release. The texturing can be painful so start with light pressure and gradually increase it.

Stretch-out Straps

These are long nylon straps with loops at the ends and along the length. They allow you to put your fingers, toes and feet into the loops so you can do the active isolated stretches discussed in Chapter 1. Brands include OPTP® and Altus® among others.

Marbles

As you can see, you will never outgrow marbles. You can get them at most toy and craft stores.

Exercise Cones

You can buy a fancy set of exercise cones or substitute other objects that are about 12 inches tall.

Equipment that Increases Resistance

Weights

Increasing resistance is simply adding weight in the direction of movement. Dumbbells, kettlebells, and medicine balls serve this purpose while allowing a wide range of motion. Many of the exercises in the sample program can be made more difficult by adding weight up to about 20 lbs. This means that you can get by with a relatively inexpensive set of dumbbells.

The most economical and convenient way to purchase dumbbells is as a set. The ones that require you to add or remove plates on the end are tedious to use. You will need dumbbells in 5-pound increments, or thereabouts, from 5 to 20 pounds. At some point, you may do other exercises that require more weight.

Kettlebells are a popular alternative to dumbbells. The handle makes them easy to use, but they are not adjustable. Like dumbbells, they can be purchased individually or as a set.

Resistance Bands

There are a wide variety of resistance bands on the market. You will need a supply of these in various shapes, sizes, and resistance levels. Some of them come in loops and some as lengths. You can often use resistance bands instead of dumbbells.

Superbands look like giant rubber bands. They are 40" long and   inch thick and come in various widths. Wider ones offer greater resistance than the narrower ones. These are ideal for squats and side-stepping exercises.

Therabands are wide, flat, thin lengths of latex that come in a large range of elasticity so they are ideal for adding incremental resistance. The ends can be tied together to create loops of various sizes or one end can be tied to a handrail or door knob to anchor it. These are useful for chops (shoulder to hip rotation), pulling motions, and side-stepping.

Resistance tubing comes in various thicknesses and levels of resistance. It usually has handles or clips at the ends so it can be anchored almost anywhere and held comfortably.

Anchoring

Some of the exercises you do with resistance bands and all of the ones done with the TRX Suspension Trainer (discussed below) require anchoring to something sturdy. The manufacturers of these products often offer doorway or wall anchors as an optional item. At first glance, these extras may seem like an unnecessary expense, but they are extremely useful and add a measure of safety (and convenience) you can't get by improvising. Paying a bit extra for the anchoring device is usually worthwhile. A single wall-mounted anchor (like the one for the TRX) can be used for the TRX and for the various resistance tubes and bands you will use. Having anchors at various heights is a plus.

Equipment that Creates Instability

Large inflated balls make exercises more difficult because you must keep the ball from rolling when you do exercises with it. Known as exercise balls, stability balls or the brand name, Swiss balls, these are the large, heavy-duty inflatable balls that you see being used in the Sample Program in Chapter 4. They vary in diameter from 45 to 75 cm (18 to 30 inches). Get the size recommended for your height and weight by the manufacturer. Generally, larger, softer balls are more stable than smaller, firmer ones.

A BOSU® Balance Trainer is basically an exercise ball cut in half and put on a platform. It can be used with the round side up or with the round side down.

TRX® Suspension Trainer by Fitness Anywhere

The TRX creates instability by suspension. There are numerous exercises in the Sample Plan that use the TRX which consists of a pair of adjustable nylon straps with handles/foot cradles at the ends. It can be attached to virtually any tall, stable object indoors or out. Either your hands or feet go into the loops and there are hundreds of exercises that can be done using your bodyweight alone. It is easy to adjust the difficulty of the exercises by adjusting the length of the straps and the amount of bodyweight you apply. This is the most useful piece of FST equipment you can buy.

*Photo 82: TRX®Suspension Trainer
Photo provided by manufacturer
and used with their permission.*

Balance Pads

Balance Pads are thick foam pads of varying firmness that you can stand on while doing various exercises. The thicker, squishier pads are more difficult to balance on than the thinner, firmer ones. Brands include AIREX® and Arma® and AeroMAT®.

Chapter 7
Injuries and Reconditioning

"But why run a marathon, you ask? Isn't it a bit of an overreaction? Running is very bad for you, everyone knows that. It does irreparable damage to your knees and lumbar vertebrae. A perfectly tolerable level of fitness can be achieved by just walking briskly for 20 minutes three times a week."

Russell Taylor, The Looniness of the Long Distance Runner

The best approach to treating injuries is to prevent them in the first place with FST and a sound training plan, but not every injury is preventable. You could step in a hole on a run and twist your ankle or fall off your bike. However, most of the injuries that plague triathletes come from overuse. These injuries develop when an abnormal load or stress is placed on a muscle, ligament or bone either directly or when the stability of the kinetic chain (linked body parts that create movement) is impaired due to weakness or misalignment.

The following overuse injuries are typically seen in triathletes. We describe them here to give you an idea of where to start if you suffer from any of these particular issues. If you have suffered from any of these problems in the past, you can get an idea where you may need to focus more attention during your strength training.

Plantar Fasciitis

What it is: Inflammation in the ligament in the bottom of the foot that connects the heel to the toes and supports the arch of your foot. It may begin as heel or arch pain and can be debilitating.

What causes it: Increased load through the foot from excessive inward (pronation) or outward (supination) roll of the foot during normal motion, or poor muscular control of the calf and hip muscles. Poor mobility through the calf that limits normal ankle motion is also a common culprit.

What to do about it: Strengthen the muscles of the foot and the hip stabilizers, and stretch the calf to decrease the load on the plantar fascia. Exercises that address these areas include Standing Marbles, the various forms of Cone Reaches and Lunges.

Achilles Tendonitis (Tendinosis)

What it is: Chronic inflammation of the Achilles tendon. However, in most cases, the condition is misnamed "tendonitis" when it is actually a biochemical change in the tendon caused by abnormal forces on it.

What causes it: Poor lower extremity mechanics and decreased coordination in the contraction of the calf muscle. The calf muscle controls motion when the foot is on the ground and as the body is moving over it. The muscle is contracting but being lengthened when doing so. This is called an eccentric contraction and when it is poorly controlled, the load on the Achilles tendon and/or calf muscles can be excessive.

What to do about it: STOP and rest. Take the load off the tendon. This is one of the more difficult injuries to work through. Once the pain has started to subside, perform calf raises on a step. Move up on your toes with both feet and then slowly lower yourself down on the painful side. Repeat this process of going up on both feet and down on the painful side for three sets of 15 repetitions.

Tibial Stress Syndrome

What it is: Commonly known as "shin splints," this condition is characterized by pain and sometimes swelling along the front inside aspect of the lower leg (tibia).

What causes it: Ramping up your training too quickly is usually the culprit, but this problem can also be cause by caused by overpronation, a tight Achilles tendon or calves, and/or weak ankle muscles.

What do to about it: Reduce the intensity of your running, ice the area after workouts. Take an anti-inflammatory. Strengthen the feet and ankles with the exercises in the Corrective Phase and see a physical therapist to determine if there is a biomechanical problem.

Patellar Tendonitis

What it is: Patellar tendonitis is an inflammation of the tendon connecting the knee cap to the lower leg (tibia) causing pain and tenderness.

What causes it: This is typically a chronic injury caused by overuse and poor biomechanics. Acute patellar tendonitis is caused by an acute blow or fall on the knee.

What to do about it: The first step in treating patellar tendonitis is rest, icing, and anti-inflammatory medication until symptoms subside. A therapeutic exercise program should be administered by a physical therapist to correct any biomechanical dysfunctions.

IT Band Syndrome

What it is: The IT band (iliotibial band) is a strip of connective tissue that runs from the hip across the outside of the knee and inserts in the tibia. The IT band becomes inflamed when there are excessive rotational loads on the band.

What causes it: Friction and loads on the IT band increase when the hip and core muscles are weak. Flat feet can also contribute to the excessive inward rotation of the leg.

What to do about it: Take the stress off the band by reducing run volume and increasing hip and core strength. Many of the exercises in the Sample Program address these areas. See Figure 11 in Chapter 5 for a list. Self-myofascial release with a foam roll is also helpful.

Hamstring Strain

What it is: A hamstring strain is an overstretching of the hamstring muscle or tendon. Symptoms include pain, tenderness, and swelling in the hamstring muscle in the back of the thigh.

What causes it: Hamstring strains are caused by over stretching of the muscle.

What to do about it: The first step in treating hamstring strains include rest, ice massage, stretching, and anti-inflammatory medication. A therapeutic exercise program administered by a physical therapist will help return strength and flexibility to the muscle. In the event of a severe hamstring strain, see your doctor.

Hip Flexor Strain

What it is: A hip flexor strain is an overstretching or overloading of the hip flexor muscle or tendon. Symptoms include pain and tenderness where the front of the thigh meets the hip bone.

What causes it: Hip Flexor Strains are caused by overstretching of muscles that lift the knee and straighten the leg (iliopsoas and rectis femoris). This can be caused by cycling and running.

What to do about it: The first step in treating hip flexor strains include rest, ice massage, stretching, and anti-inflammatory medication. A therapeutic exercise program administered by a physical therapist will help return strength and flexibility to the muscles. In the event of a severe hip flexor strain, see your doctor.

Shoulder Impingement

What it is: Impingement refers to mechanical compression and/or wear of the rotator cuff tendons. The rotator cuff is comprised of four muscles connecting the shoulder blade (scapula) to the upper part of the shoulder joint (humeral head). Normally, the rotator cuff glides smoothly between the undersurface of the acromion (a part of the shoulder blade); however, in the case of impingement, this space narrows and the tissues become irritated.

What causes it: Anything that interferes with this normal gliding can lead to impingement. This can happen due to aging, overuse or an acute injury. The most common cause is poor posture and poor shoulder blade mechanics.

When the tendon weakens and degenerates due to aging, it can cause the formation of bone spurs and/or inflammatory tissue within the space above the rotator cuff (subacromial space). Swimming and poor running posture can lead to overuse impingements in triathletes. Acute injuries, such as falling off your bike, can create impingements too.

What to do about it: The first step is to temporarily avoid the activities that seem to be causing the problem. A non-steroidal anti-inflammatory medication, such as Aleve, may also be recommended by your doctor. A therapeutic exercise program administered by a physical therapist can correct posture and treat the impingement. Surgery is usually not necessary, but if symptoms persist despite adequate non-surgical treatment, it may be beneficial.

Getting Better and Better

Making FST part of your life will be one of the best things you ever did. Your medicine chest will get dusty and your race times will improve. You will begin to experience benefits right away, but like most things, the greatest gains come with patience and persistence. It is time to get started.

Chapter 8
Advanced Exercises

Integrating Motion

The Functional Strength Exercises in the book are recommended because their basic mechanics (not necessarily their appearance) corresponds to the target activities of swimming, biking and running. They are mulitplanar movements requiring stability through key transfer stations (the ankle, hip, core and shoulders) that engage kinetic chains important in triathlon (single leg propulsion and shoulder to hip rotation).

You will recall from earlier discussion that Proprioceptors are the specialized nerve receptors that carry sensory information from the skin, muscles and joints to the brain. They tell our brain among other things, where we are in space, how fast a joint and/or muscle is moving, how much tension a muscle and tendon is developing.

We can illustrate their importance by looking at what happens when they don't work. Have you ever woken up in the middle of the night and your whole foot or leg was asleep? It is completely numb and when you stand up you can't feel your foot, and you don't know where your leg is? That is what happens when the position you are sleeping in compresses a nerve and blocks the transmission of sensory information from the proprioceptors in the skin, muscles and joints to your brain. Trying to walk will be nearly impossible until you change positions so the impulses can make it back to your brain.

In contrast, let's look at what happens when proprioception is intact as you run. When your foot hits the ground the arch collapses slightly (pronation) and the ankle bends as you come over the top. This motion at the foot and ankle stimulates the pacinian corpuscles (which detect speed in the change of the joints), raffini endings (which detect change in the angle of the joint) the muscle spindle (which detects the length of the calf muscles) and the golgi tendons (which detect force in the Achilles tendon). All this information is sent up to your brain for processing.

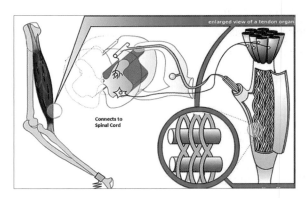

Figure 13: Golgi Tendon

After the information is processed, signals are sent back down to the appropriate muscles telling them to contract. The more numerous and precise the signals coming up from the foot, the more efficient the response can be going back down to it. The Sample Program was a solid start, but now we want to work more on the finer point of integration. That is, to integrate the improved function of these proprioceptors with the improved muscle strength and coordination you started developing with the FST Sample Program. Gary Gray, P.T., summarizes this integration as "load and explode" and it is the basis for optimal movement. In this chapter we will show you some exercises that will optimize the integration of proprioception with action.

Integration Exercises

The following exercises are specialized movement patterns of varying degrees of difficulty that move you along various planes of motion. Their purpose is to improve muscle integration. These exercises are identified in figure 14 by the discipline they target.

Figure 14: Table of Integration Exercises by Discipline

45 ° lunge	all
90° lunge	all
135° lunge	all
45° lunge with arm drive	all
90° lunge with arm drive	all
135° lunge with arm drive	all
Single leg 45° reach forward	all
Single leg 45° reach back	all
Single leg back reach	all
Single leg side reach	all
Single leg forward reach	all
Single leg side reach left	all
Forward Lunge	all
Forward Lunge arm drive	all
BosuBall long "T"	swim
BosuBall long "Y"	swim
BosuBall thoracic rotation	swim

Prone BosuBall® Balance	swim
Tether swimming	swim
Bike Pivot Prone	bike
Bike long extension start	bike
Bike long extension end	bike
Bike rotation	bike
Bike long "Y"	bike
A skips	bike
B skips	run
Leg Drives	run
Parachute/Bungee running	run

Instructions for Integration Exercises

This group of exercises can be completed after your dynamic warm-up, before any of your cardiovascular work-outs or in conjunction with your strength training session. Do the discipline-specific exercises if you need an extra boost in that particular leg of the race.

The photos are self explanatory. The important thing to remember is that our aim is to stimulate proprioceptors. Therefore the *direction* of the movement pattern is just as important as the execution of the movement.

We will start with a series of lunges and reaches that will benefit every triathlon discipline. They are set up in a bisected grid pattern. You can create such a pattern on the floor using masking tape set up in a congifuration with 45°, 90° and 135° angles like those in figure 13.

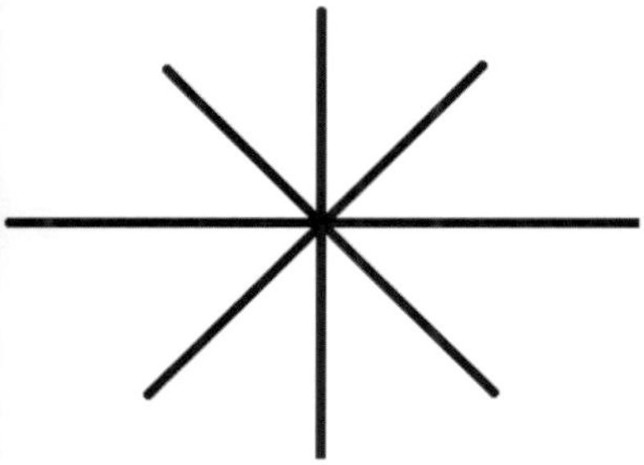

Figure 15: Bisected Grid Pattern for Integration Exercises

Each one becomes more challenging as the complexity of the movement pattern increases. Make your step and lower your body weight, then spring back to the starting position, keeping in mind the concept of "load and explode". Get into a rhythm and repeat the motion for ten repetitions then go immediately into the next exercise in the sequence.

The exercises that contribute to overall integration (they benefit every discipline) are:

- Lunges at various angles
- Lunges with arm drive
- Single leg reaches
- Forward lunges

Multi-directional Lunges:

Photo 84: 90° Lunge

Photo 83: 45° Lunge

Photo 85: 135° Lunge

Multi-directional Lunges with arm drive:

Photo 86: 45° Lunge with Arm Drive

Photo 87: 90° Lunge with Arm Drive

Photo 88: 135° Lunge with Arm Drive

Single-leg with reach:

Photo 89: Single Leg 45° with Reach Forward

Photo 90: Single Leg 45° with Reach Back

Integration Exercises for Swimming

Maintaining stability and body position is key to maximizing power output and minimizing drag in the water. Start with the arms in the position pictured but lower to the ground. The exercise is lifting the weight (or rotating the shoulders) higher off the ground. The integration exercises for swimming include:

- BosuBall® "T" and "Y"
  - BosuBall® thoracic rotation
  - BosuBall® balance
  - Tether swimming (not pictured but described below)

Photo 91: BosuBall® "T"

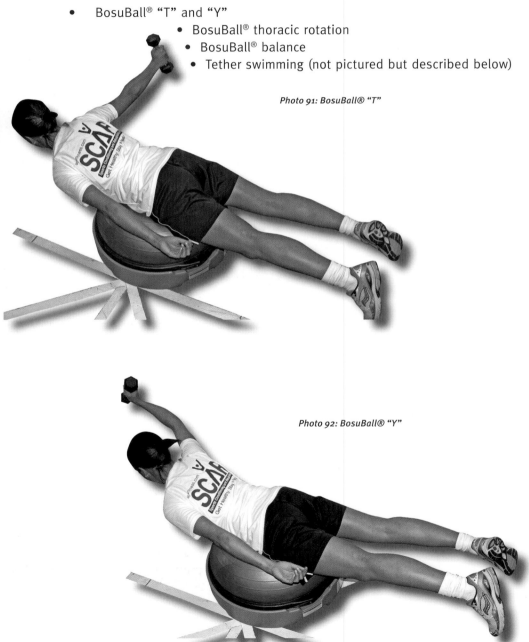

Photo 92: BosuBall® "Y"

Photo 93: BosuBall® thoracic rotation

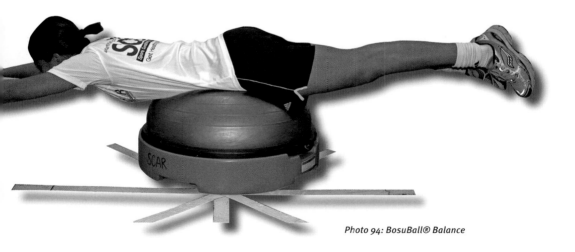

Photo 94: BosuBall® Balance

Tether Swimming

The strength building exercises commonly prescribed for swimmers are pathetically inadequate because they focus on shoulder strength while ignoring the real powerhouse, body rotation. Tether swimming is an excellent tool for integrating the functional strength you have developed in the gym. When swimming against a tether (which is fastened at your waist and anchored to a handrail or something behind the swimmer) you encounter resistance in every phase of the swimming movement, including body rotation.

That said, it is important to use tether swimming carefully. Start out with just a few repetitions (maybe 3 sets of 50 strokes) and build slowly to longer set of up to 200 strokes/repetitions. Use the tether no more than once a week for short periods, the same as you would do short running intervals at very high speed.

Use the right tether

A tether should create resistance as you move forward in your normal swimming position. Getting the body position right is complicated because triathletes wear wetsuits on race day. So ideally, a triathlete will practice often in a wetsuit and will wear the wetsuit while doing tether work too. If that isn't practical, then a tether that allows you to swim in a wetsuit-like body position is best.

Some tether systems attach at the foot or ankle. These discourage a motor-like kick which is an added benefit for triathletes that have not yet learned to use their legs judiciously during the swim.

Other tethers fasten at the waist. The ones that have a single attachment in the center of the back allow free body rotation. Swimmers that need to develop their rotational power may consider a system that attaches on each side of the waist like the AquaVee® which creates resistance during the rotation phase.

Some tethers also have flotation in the attachment belt. This improves body position for most swimmers, moving them closer to the optimal wetsuit-like position.

The anchoring system must be such that the swimmer applies force in the correct direction. There are various anchoring systems for swim tethers. Some of them attach to a pole at the end of the pool, others attach to the side of the pool or to the lane lines (StretchCordz Stationary Swim Trainer). A tether that is anchored above the swimmer is not as effective as one that is anchored directly behind him because a tall anchor point will resist movement forward and down as in Photo 95.

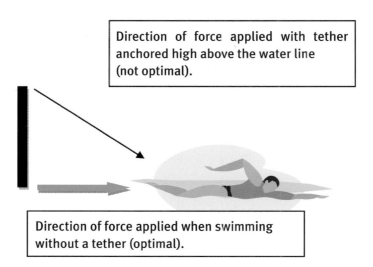

Direction of force applied with tether anchored high above the water line (not optimal).

Direction of force applied when swimming without a tether (optimal).

Figure 16: Direction of Force applied with tether anchored above swimmer

Some tethers aren't anchored at all. Rather they attach the swimmer to a small parachute which opens as the swimmer moves forward. If you have a buddy, you can tether to another swimmer so you can engage in a tug of war. The tug of war is effective for both of the attached swimmers, no matter what their skill level. The longer the tug of war lasts, the better the workout.

Photo 95 : StretchCordz®Short Belt Tether. Photo provided by and use with permission of manufacturer".

Integration Exercises for Cycling

Power for cycling comes from strong rotational core control on each pedal stroke. You will increase power to your legs by maintaining stability and support through the opposite arm and shoulder. Try these exercises during those long winter months when you are stuck on the trainer.

- Bike pivot prone
- Bike rotation
- Bike long extension
- Bike long "Y"
- Single-leg pedaling (not pictured but described below)

Photo 96: Bike Pivot Prone

Photo 97: Bike Rotation

Photo 98: Bike Long Extension

Photo 99: Bike Long "Y"

Single–leg pedaling

Single-leg pedaling teaches you to apply pressure through the entire pedaling cycle and it also teaches you to apply more power with your less dominant leg. Your cycling shoes will tell a story if you let them. Remove the insole and examine it to see which leg you push harder with. Just imagine how much faster you could be if you got your other leg on board.

The secret to single leg pedaling is to work into it gradually and to choose the right gearing. In the beginning it is more important to stay engaged with the pedal for the entire 360° spin than it is to pedal fast or generate a lot of power. If the tension is too light (gear is too easy) you will have trouble moving quickly enough to keep tension on the pedals during the upstroke. If it is too hard (gear is too high) you will be able to stay connected but your muscles will overload very quickly. Find the sweet spot between the extremes that allows you to practice full revolutions. Start with just 10 with each leg then increase until you can do 30 seconds easily with one leg.

This is an exercise you can do on the road as well. I find that it is easier to work into this drill by starting with a higher gear on a slight decline. This way the rotation speed is slower and less power is required because of the slight downhill.

Photo 100: A Skips

Photo 101: B Skips

Integration Exercises for Running

Efficient running requires coordinated movement of your head, shoulders, arms, trunk, hips knees, ankles and feet. The following exercises will help refine the integration of these components to increase your speed, power and strength to get you up those challenging hills and through the finishing chute.

- Skips – There are two versions of this. A skips are done with a bent knee and B skips are done with a straight leg.
- Leg drives
- Resisted running (not pictured but described below)

Photo 102: Leg Drives

Resisted Running

Runners practicing for the famous and extreme "Badwater" ultramarathon are known to drag heavy ropes, chains and even tires behind them as they train. Because the runner is having to pull the object behind him it seems that this would be a very functional exercise but having something that is tether at the waist (or shoulders) requires the runner to apply force in a slightly uphill direction. This is not how force is applied in normal running.

If you really want a functional running workout, attach yourself to a parachute which trails behind you or a resistance-band (or bungee) tether anchored so that you will have to apply force forward (not upward) in order to propel yourself.

If you are training with others, the runner can pull against a buddy holding the tether. This high-intensity workout will help bring you to the next level in running.

The tether can also be reversed so that the runner is pulled forward ("speed assisted"), forcing his legs to turnover more quickly than is natural for him. This imprints faster movement patterns and is also beneficial.

Chapter 9
Ask the Expert

Question:
Why does form matter so much in strength training?

Practice doesn't make perfect. Perfect practice makes perfect. If you don't do the movement correctly you are simply reinforcing poor movement patterns. You may get fatigued but you won't change or improve anything. You have to do the exercises correctly in order to establish a functionally strong movement pattern. The most common correction I make is telling people to keep their hips up when they do certain exercises. Without fail, doing them with proper form is significantly more difficult, so if you think a particular exercise is easy, you are probably doing it wrong. That is one of the reasons it is so important to do the exercises in front of a full length mirror. Be sure to check your form.

Question:
Triathletes get little niggles all the time. At what point should an athlete seek medical help with pain? Should they go to their doctor or to a physical therapist?

Triathletes should seek help when performance is impacted. When you can't complete a workout because of pain, especially for a couple of days in a row, then it is time to see someone.

I think that many athletes don't realize that they can make an appointment with a physical therapist directly. Since doctors and physical therapists work closely together, you will be directed appropriately no matter who you go to first. If you have a nagging issue (as opposed to suffering an accident like a fall) it may be more direct to go to a physical therapist first.

Question:
Why go to a phyisical therapist rather than simply rest, ice and take aspirin?

First of all, we know that triathletes aren't very good at resting. Even if they take a few days off, they will be back at it soon, probably too soon. The most common type of injury sustained by a triathlete is an overuse injury. When you let the area rest, it produces scar tissue as it heals. When the athlete gets back to training, the scar tissue reduces the suppleness of the structure so it doesn't function as well as it once did. Other parts of the body compensate for this reduced function and now you are compensating with other muscles and you are on your way to creating an overuse injury somewhere else.

Treating the injury early will reduce the amount of scar tissue and will allow the area to heal in a way that will restore it to full function as much as possible. With select therapy the whole kinetic chain is targeted by exercise so that the entire system will be more robust. Physical therapy provides a more comprehensive and long term solution than rest and aspirin.

Question:
There are plenty of triathletes that never set foot in a gym. Are they courting disaster?

I wouldn't use the word "disaster" so much as "limitation". At some point every triathlete will encounter a weakness that will limit his ability to train and race. Some athletes, especially the younger ones, can go on for a while without being sidelined but eventually time will catch up with them and they will have to take steps to correct problems that have grown worse with time and age. I prefer to say that FST will prolong a triathlete's participation.

Question:
The utility of running shoes has become a subject of controversy. What do you think about "minimalist shoes", barefoot running and the like?

There are third-world countries where people are running significant mileage barefoot, simply because they don't own shoes. As such, I'm not going to say that running barefoot is bad. However, most people who will be reading this book have probably been wearing shoes for most of their life and to suddenly go to a minimalist shoe or to barefoot for a run may be a recipe for disaster because it is so much different than what they are used to, setting them up for injury. I also find that the athletes most attracted to this approach are those that feel that their running needs a lot of improvement so they are a vulnerable population to begin with.

That said, I have people train in minimalist shoes or barefoot on soft surfaces for the purpose of training their running mechanics. If you run on the beach, you can run in the soft sand or the hard, wet sand next to the water. Soft-sand running is difficult because the surface gives way when you apply pressure so it really forces you to be light on your feet if you want to move forward. The wet, hard sand at the water's edge is much easier but be careful to avoid running on a canted surface. Sand running has been studied to some degree on trotter horses and at least for them, running on a soft surface shortens stride length and increases stride frequency.

I think there are some definite opportunities for improved function with the right type of barefoot training. What is the right kind? Think of barefoot running

but the benefits go far beyond that. Set the speed very slow, in the realm of 1 or 2 miles per hour as you work. This is slow enough that you won't break a sweat and the walking will be almost unconscious. Desk jockeys can cover more than 25 miles per week this way.

Question:
Is running with weights a functional exercise?
Carrying extra weight during activity provides a cardiovascular challenge. The added weight increases the amount of effort your muscles make, the amount of energy they use and the speed at which they consume oxygen. This does not improve movement patterns like FST does.

Now you might say that running with extra weight must be a functional strength move because you are doing the thing you want to improve (rather than isolating just one component of it). This is true but if you carry weight when you run, the resistance is only increased in one direction: movement up and down. This is true whether you carry the weight in your hands, put it on your ankles (which is awful for your knees and hip joints by the way) or wear a weighted vest.

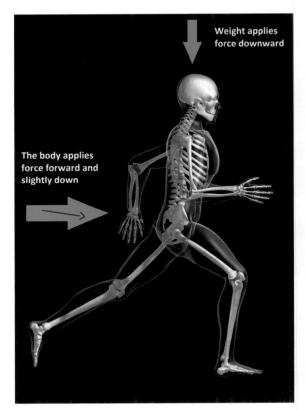

Weight applies force downward

The body applies force forward and slightly down

Figure 17: Why a weighted vest is not a functional exercise for running

Running against a tether or a parachute are effective ways to add resistance to running. Either method will build running strength and power. Running against resistance is excellent for building running strength and power. Tether exercises are among the advanced exercises described in Chapter 9.

Appendix A
Functional Strength Assessment

The best FST program is one that is designed around your goals and current abilities. This test will only take a few minutes and is designed to find areas of weakness that are relevant to swimming, biking, and running. As a triathlete, you probably feel confident that you are reasonably fit and strong but chances are good that you will find some problem areas.

Use the results of this test to help you plan your Functional Strength Program. If you pass the test, you need only spend a week or two in the Corrective Phase. If you fail in multiple areas, you will have to invest more time in the Corrective Phase.

The Sample Program already targets all of the areas tested in this assessment. However, you should make sure that each Functional Strength Training Phase includes more than one exercise that focuses on your problem areas. If you have to add more exercises to address an area of weakness, feel free to do so. Use Figure 11 in Chapter 5 to find appropriate exercises.

This test has three parts:
1. Strength Assessment
2. Balance Assessment
3. Flexibility Assessment

How to perform the test:
- All movements should be done with your shoes off in front of a large mirror.
- You will need an armless chair or bench and a doorway.
- Each movement must be done correctly to receive a passing mark.
- If you can only do the movement in a compromised position, we call that a "compensation." The compensation indicates an area of weakness that needs attention. The muscle groups that need attention are indicated on the corresponding chart. Exercises for those muscle groups can be found in Chapter 4.
- Use the chart to evaluate yourself as you do the movement.
- It is helpful to have a partner who can assist you.

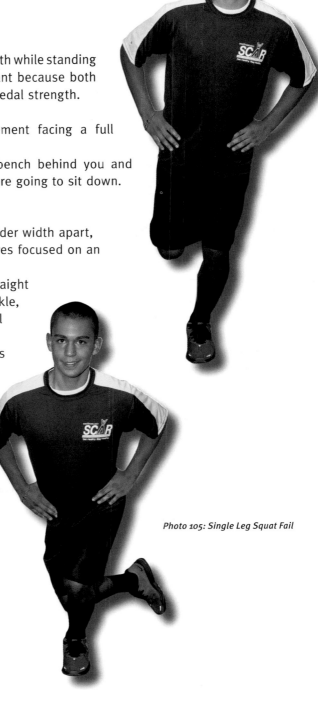

Test # 1:
STRENGTH ASSESSMENT

Single Leg Squat

The single leg squat tests strength while standing on a single leg. This is important because both running and cycling require bipedal strength.

Procedure: Perform the movement facing a full length mirror.
Position an armless chair or bench behind you and stand in front of it as if you were going to sit down.

Position:

1. Stand with your feet shoulder width apart, hands on your hips and eyes focused on an object straight ahead.
2. Feet should be pointed straight forward with your foot, ankle, knee, and hips in a neutral position.
3. Raise one foot a few inches off the floor in front of you with a straight knee.

Movement:

4. Squat to a comfortable level, then return to starting position.
5. Perform five repetitions, then switch legs.

Photo 105: Single Leg Squat Fail

Strength Test	Correct movement looks like...	OK Left?	OK Right?	If the athlete compensates with...	Then the cause is Tight Musculature...	and/or Weak Musculature
Single Leg Squat	Neutral foot			Ankle and foot rolls inward, foot flattens	Calf	Arch musculature
	Knee forward & over foot			Knees move inward	Hip, hamstrings, quadriceps	Gluteus muscles, quadriceps
	Even hips			Hip drop	N/A	Gluteus medius
	Vertical trunk			Trunk sway	Hips, hamstrings, quadriceps	Gluteus muscles, quadriceps

Core Strength

This test has four positions. It is best to have a partner view you from the side to look for compensations.

Position 1 – Plank

Position:
- Perform a plank by bringing your body up onto your elbows and toes. Do not let the hips sag nor allow them to be higher than your shoulders.

Photo 106: Plank Pass

Photo 107: Plank Fail

Position 2 – Plank with leg lift

Position:

- Perform a plank by bringing your body up onto your elbows and toes. Do not let the hips sag nor allow them to be higher than your shoulders.

Movement:

- Lift up your right leg off the floor without twisting your body or your hips. Return to the starting position, then pick up your left leg.
- Keep your body in a straight line. Do not let your hips sag.
- Return to the starting position, then repeat, lifting the right leg.

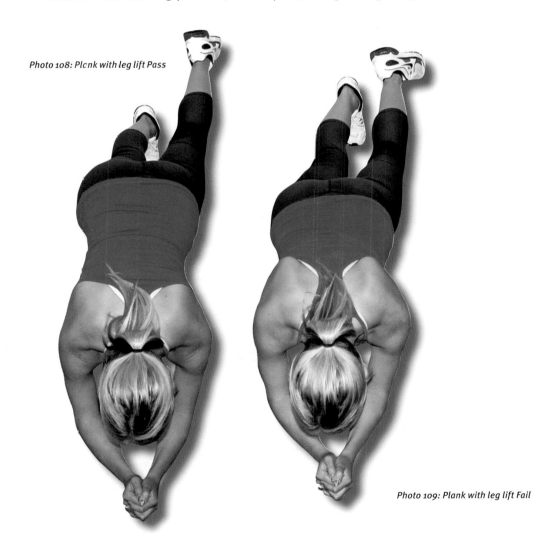

Photo 108: Plank with leg lift Pass

Photo 109: Plank with leg lift Fail

Position 3 – Plank with arm reach
Position:
- Perform a plank by bringing your body up onto your elbows and toes. Do not let the hips sag nor allow them to be higher than your shoulders.

Movement:
- Reach your right arm forward. Return to starting position and reach your left arm forward.
- Keep your body in a straight line. Do not let your hips sag.
- Return to the starting position, then repeat, lifting the right arm.

Position 4 – Plank with arm reach and leg lift
Position:
- Perform a plank by bringing your body up onto your elbows and toes. Do not let the hips sag nor allow them to be higher than your shoulders.

Movement:
- Reach your right arm forward and lift your left leg up.
- Hold the position, keeping your body in a straight line. Do not let your hips sag.
- Return to starting position, then reach your left arm forward and lift your right leg up.

Core Strength Tests	Correct movement looks like......	OK?	If the athlete compensates with...
Plank with Full Body Rotation	Straight back		Sagging back
	Body remains aligned from line shoulder to foot		Dropping hip to floor
Plank with Right/Left Leg Lift	Straight back		Arched back
	No lateral shift		Lateral shift left
	No trunk rotation		Left/right trunk rotation
Plank with Right/Left Arm Reach	Straight back		Arched back
	No lateral shift		Lateral shift left
	No trunk rotation		Left /right trunk rotation Left/right scapular winging
Plank with Right Arm Reach & Left/Right Leg Lift	Straight back		Arched back
	No lateral shift		Lateral shift right
	No trunk rotation		Left /right trunk rotation

Photo 110: Plank with Arm Lift and Leg Lift Pass

Photo 110: Plank with Arm Lift and Leg Lift Pass

Photo 111: Plank with Arm lift and Leg Lift Fail

Test # 2:
BALANCE ASSESSMENT

Single Leg Balance Test
Begin standing on the floor with your feet facing forward.

Movement:
- Lift one foot off the floor about 3 inches and see how long you can keep your balance.
- Repeat with opposite foot.

BALANCE TEST	Leg tested	How long can you keep your balance?	Balance time to pass this test
Single Leg Balance Test	Left Leg		30-60 seconds
	Right Leg		30-60 seconds
Single Leg Balance Test (with eyes closed)	Left Leg		30-60 seconds
	Right Leg		30-60 seconds

Test # 3:
FLEXIBILITY ASSESSMENT

Straight Leg Raise

The straight leg raise assesses hamstring flexibility.

Starting Position:
- Begin by lying on your back in a doorway with both legs straight. Hip should be aligned with the door jamb.

Movement:
- Perform a straight leg raise, keeping the opposite leg flat on the ground and the leg in the air straight with the foot flexed (not pointed).

Views:
- This test should be viewed from the side.

FLEXIBILITY TEST	Correct motion is...	If the athlete compensates with...	Then it indicates...
Straight Leg Raise	Foot of the straight, raised leg should be able to touch the door jamb	Foot unable to reach the door jamb	Hamstring tightness

Photo 112: Straight Leg Raise Pass

Photo 113: Straight Leg Raise Fail

Index

A

Abdominals 24, 85, 90
Active Isolated Stretching 13
Aerobars 127
Aerobic Training 93
Anchoring, suspension trainer 98
Anchoring, tether 114
Angels 42
Ankle support 125
Atomic push-up 65, 90

B

Back Rotation Lunge 63, 90
Backstroke 42
Balance 96, 98-99, 108
Balance assesment 136
Barefoot running 123
Bench Press 11
Bicep Curl 71, 90
Bike, exercises for
(see also Cycling) 25, 33, 108, 116
Biomotor abilities 30
BosuBall 107, 112
BosuBall Push-up 81, 89, 91
Brick, aerobic and strength 38, 93, 126
Bungee running exercise 108, 120

C

Cable chops 62, 90
Calf roll out 43
Calf sleeve 125
Calories 126
Chest Press 21, 69, 90
Compression garments 125
Cone reach 76, 91
Cones 76, 77, 79, 82, 91, 97
Cook, Gray 23
Core, muscles comprising 15, 23-24, 38, 43
Corrective exercise 38, 43
Corrective phase 38, 44, 102, 130
Cycling 112, 130

D

Drinking bird 15

E

Endurance Exercise 63, 90

Endurance Strength 39, 90
Energy Leak 23
Equipment 95
Exercise matt 96

F

Foam roller 21, 43, 92, 96
Freestyle pull 84, 91
FST 10
Fueling for strength workout 126
Functional strength 10
Functional strength training phases 36

G

Glutes (gluteus maximus) 47
Gluteus medius 23, 122
Golgi tendon 106

H

Hamstring stretch 20, 35
Hamstring trio 52
Heel strike 124
Hills 33, 119
Hip flexor 16, 103, 127

I

Inch worm 18
Injury 101
Injury rates 32
Injury, prevention of 23, 31
Instability 23, 25, 92, 96, 98
Integration exercises 107
Ironman 32, 125
IT band (Illiotibial band) 13, 21, 43, 103

J

Jumping 124

K

Kettlebells 97
Kinesio taping 125
Kinetic chain 23, 27, 101, 106, 123

L

Leg cradle 14
Longevity in sport 32
Lunge exercises 17, 54, 62, 63, 72, 73, 78
Lunge hop 78, 91
Lunge, Integration 109